Pride and Prejudice

Jane Austen

Guide written and developed by
John Mahoney and Stewart Martin

Charles Letts & Co Ltd
London, Edinburgh & New York

First published 1987
by Charles Letts & Co Ltd
Diary House, Borough Road, London SE1 1DW
Reprinted 1988

Illustration: Peter McClure

Stewart Martin is an Honours graduate of Lancaster University, where he read English
and Sociology. He has worked both in the UK and abroad as a writer, a teacher, and an
educational consultant. He is married with three children, and is currently deputy
headmaster at Ossett School in West Yorkshire.

John Mahoney has taught English for twenty years. He has been head of English
department in three schools and has wide experience of preparing students at all levels
for most examination boards. He has worked both in the UK and North America
producing educational books and computer software on English language and literature.
He is married with three children and lives in Worcestershire.

British Library Cataloguing in Publication Data
Mahoney, John
Pride and prejudice, Jane Austen
(Guides to literature)
I. Austen, Jane. Pride and prejudice.
I. Title   II. Martin, Stewart
III. Austen, Jane   IV. Series
823'.7   PR4034.P7

ISBN 0 85097 763 0

Printed and bound in Great Britain by
Charles Letts (Scotland) Ltd

Contents

To the student

This study companion to your English literature text acts as a guide to the novel or play being studied. It suggests ways in which you can explore content and context, and focuses your attention on those matters which will lead to an understanding, appreciative and sensitive response to the work of literature being studied.

Whilst covering all those aspects dealt with in the traditional-style study aid, more importantly, it is a flexible companion to study, enabling you to organize the patterns of study and priorities which reflect your particular needs at any given moment.

Whilst in many places descriptive, it is never prescriptive, always encouraging a sensitive personal response to a work of literature, rather than the shallow repetition of others' opinions. Such objectives have always been those of the good teacher, and have always assisted the student to gain high grades in 16+ examinations in English literature. These same factors are also relevant to students who are doing coursework in English literature for the purposes of continual assessment.

The major part of this guide is the 'Commentary' where you will find a detailed commentary and analysis of all the important things you should know and study for your examination. There is also a section giving practical help on how to study a set text, write the type of essay that will gain high marks, prepare coursework and a guide to sitting examinations.

Used sensibly, this guide will be invaluable in your studies and help ensure your success in the course.

Jane Austen

Jane Austen was born in 1775, the seventh of eight children, in Steventon, Hampshire, where her father was rector. Although not rich, it was an upper-class family, and her six brothers all took up professions befitting their class, either in the Church or the armed services.

Jane and her sister Cassandra were largely educated at home by their parents, apart from a three-year stint at boarding school in Oxford and Reading when they were quite young. The children were encouraged to read widely and Jane was well-versed in the literature of the 18th century.

Although she lived at a time when the Romantic movement flourished, she did not share with Keats, Shelley and Byron the same interest in passion and emotion. Instead her work reflected the classical ideals of order and reason that were common in the earlier part of the 18th century.

Jane Austen's world was small, somewhat narrow and mainly rural. Despite frequent journeys to Kent, London and Bath, her life remained largely untouched by the events of the outside world. The industrial revolution, which caused vast changes to many parts of Britain, and the wars in Europe at that time, did not seem to impinge unduly. They certainly do not have a place in her writing. Instead Jane is concerned chiefly with moral and intellectual questions which she explores within the limits of a small number of closely observed characters. She stays very much within the social class with which she is familiar. Her characters have backgrounds similar to her own. This does not prevent her, however, from depicting characters of great depth and interest, or from commenting both wittily and intelligently on human nature as she sees it.

Having 'scribbled' frequently as a child, Jane began writing seriously at the age of twenty-one in 1796. Her first work was originally entitled *First Impressions*, but having no success with a publisher, was redrafted at a later date and finally published as *Pride and Prejudice* in 1813. She wrote two other manuscripts at this time, but they also remained unpublished until later.

Jane still lived at home, unmarried, and in 1801 the family moved to Bath on Mr Austen's retirement. Despite frequent travel, Jane did not enjoy town life very much. It seems that during this period she did no further writing and it was not until she returned with her mother to live once more in Hampshire that she took up writing again.

Jane became very ill in 1816 and, although she was taken to Winchester in search of the best medical help, she died there in 1817 at the age of forty-one.

Jane Austen's work is admired and appreciated for the skill in plot construction and character description, and the subtlety of dialogue. All three qualities are admirably displayed in *Pride and Prejudice*.

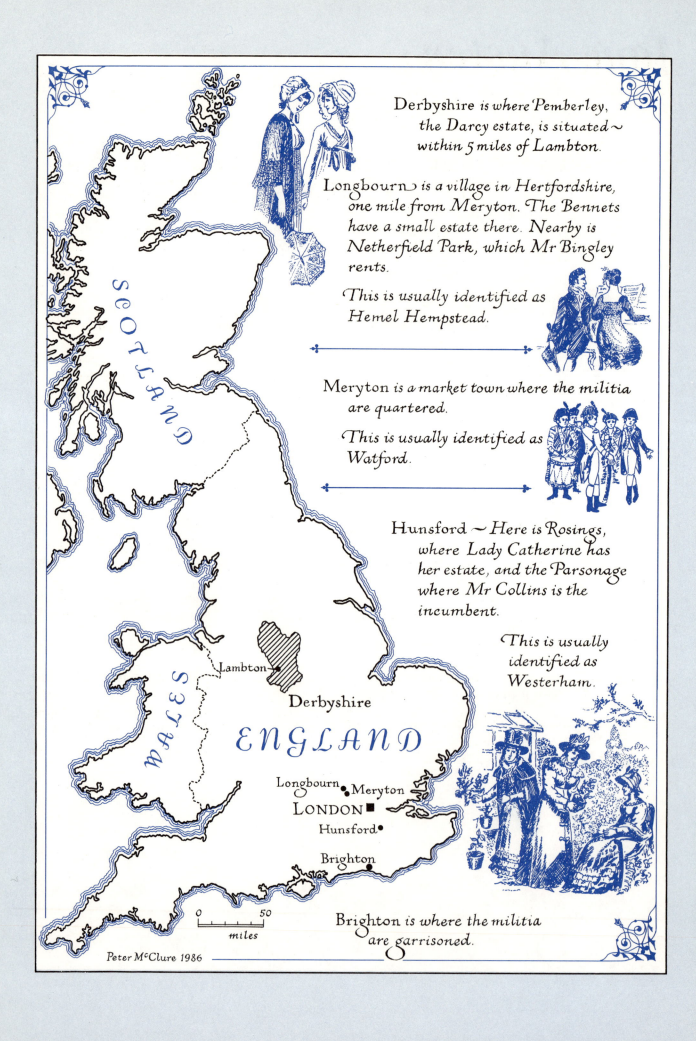

Derbyshire *is where* Pemberley, *the Darcy estate, is situated ~ within 5 miles of* Lambton.

Longbourn *is a village in* Hertfordshire, *one mile from* Meryton. *The Bennets have a small estate there. Nearby is* Netherfield Park, *which Mr Bingley rents.*

This is usually identified as Hemel Hempstead.

Meryton *is a market town where the militia are quartered.*

This is usually identified as Watford.

Hunsford ~ *Here is* Rosings, *where Lady Catherine has her estate, and the Parsonage where Mr Collins is the incumbent.*

This is usually identified as Westerham.

SCOTLAND

WALES

ENGLAND

Lambton

Derbyshire

Longbourn • Meryton
LONDON ■
Hunsford •

Brighton •

0   50
miles

Brighton *is where the militia are garrisoned.*

Peter McClure 1986

Understanding Pride and Prejudice

An exploration of the major topics and themes in the novel

Summaries of themes

Aspects of language

Jane Austen's versatility in her use of language is reflected in the many differences of personality revealed in her characters. The rambling, senseless speech of Mrs Bennet is different from Darcy's measured, considered language. Mr Collins's pomposity is revealed through his language. His laborious list of reasons for marrying Elizabeth is an example of this. Jane Austen is also adept at singling out the phrase or word which best describes or satirizes her characters. Hence she ridicules Mr Collins's false modesty with the repetition of 'humble abode' or underlines Miss Bingley's hypocrisy with words such as 'sweet' or 'dear'.

Dialogue She uses dialogue most skilfully to show character. Mr and Mrs Bennet reveal much about themselves and their relationship to each other through dialogue. We get to know Mr Collins through the absurdity of his speeches. The contrast in character between Jane and Elizabeth is revealed through their discussion of Bingley's absence. Dialogue is also a great source of humour. Mr Bennet's sarcasm, Mr Collins's foolishness, Elizabeth's wit and perspicacity are all revealed through conversation. Dialogue adds a dramatic note to the story, as witnessed by the conversation after Darcy's proposal, or Lady de Bourgh's interview with Elizabeth at Longbourn. Dialogue is realistic and brings the characters to life. Jane Austen uses it thoughtfully and sometimes refrains from using it where you might most expect it, for example, Darcy's proposal is actually in reported speech. Very often she uses dialogue to expand a point of character she has already made, thus underlining the particular characteristic.

Irony Jane Austen sets the tone, as well as the theme of her book, in the first sentence when she implies that it is not so much the young men who are 'in want of a wife' as the families with daughters who are choosing them! The irony in the book is revealed by the skilful choice of the correct word. Hence Miss Bingley's hypocrisy is summed up when she describes Jane and Elizabeth as 'dear friends'; Lady de Bourgh's lack of breeding is noted when she is called 'this great lady'. Irony is also revealed through dialogue. The final conversation between Elizabeth and Wickham is full of implicit meaning as she lets him know that she is fully aware of the truth about him.

So cleverly has Jane Austen constructed the novel that she is able to use dramatic irony to great effect. Look at Elizabeth's comment that Charlotte would never marry for money, or Bingley's comment that he considers himself 'fixed at Netherfield', or the way Mr Collins believes himself valued at Rosings. Most ironic of all is Elizabeth's statement to Darcy about the necessity of being certain in one's judgment before making up one's mind about someone!

Wit One of the strongest elements of the book is the large seam of humour that runs through it. Elizabeth with her 'lively, playful disposition' is able to make jokes at her own expense as well as other people's. She is able to laugh at Darcy's insult at Netherfield and turn it into a funny story to amuse her friends. She makes light of potentially embarrassing situations, as when she is excluded by the narrowness of the path from walking with Darcy and the Bingley sisters, or when her mother is talking too much at Netherfield. She jokes about the fuss made when Miss de Bourgh arrives at Hunsford. Her conversations with Darcy are alive with wit, she gently teasing his seriousness and pride. It is in front of Darcy that she acknowledges she is at her cleverest. He is the 'spur' to her 'genius'. She uses wit to cover her own embarrassment as when Darcy asks her to dance. She covers the silences with humorous remarks about the accepted need for conversation.

Elizabeth does, however, resort to sarcasm, as when she is ridiculing Darcy's snobbery or Mr Collins's obsequiousness. Much of the wit of the book is sarcastic. Mr Bennet, in particular, uses it as a weapon to defend himself against the pettiness of his wife and most of his daughters, as well as to indulge his pleasure in the absurd at the expense of such characters as Mr Collins.

'I hope I never ridicule what is wise or good.' These words apply equally well to Jane Austen as they do to Elizabeth. She ridicules the faults in her characters – Miss Bingley's and Darcy's snobbery; Mrs Bennet's insensitivity; Lady de Bourgh's domineering quality; Mr Collins's lack of aesthetic appreciation and superficiality of feeling; Sir William Lucas's obsequiousness. She mocks the general assumptions of public opinion, as shown best, perhaps, in the opening sentence of the book. She also ridicules society's hypocrisy and fickleness.

Social aspects

Background   Jane Austen was writing in the early 19th century about the landed gentry of southern England. She does not go into great detail about social or political background as she was concerned almost entirely with the way people behaved towards each other. The people of her book enjoy a comfortable, leisurely life, often moving from the gaiety of London in the winter to their country residences in the summer. There they pursue sports and hold parties and balls. The activities of the ladies are limited, and education informal. Music, drawing and dancing are among the accomplishments regarded as useful. Those who are not wealthy enough to own town residences have to rely on occasional visits to London and other towns to relieve the dullness of country life.

Jane Austen looks at her world satirically. She mocks the snobbery, hypocrisy and materialism of many of the people, as well as their narrow view of life. She also states though, through the character of Elizabeth, that, despite these restrictions, this society can produce a person of lively wit and intelligence.

Class   Jane Austen deals almost exclusively with one class – the landed gentry. She describes in detail their attitudes, social behaviour, and their preoccupations. They are a tight-knit group who are bound by strict codes of conduct which do not easily admit new members. They are snobbish and mercenary as well as being censorious of those who contravene social and moral standards. Anyone who does breach the barricades is portrayed as unctuous and obsequious.

Theirs is a society where the individual is seen as very much part of a wider group. He must consider the wishes and interests of family and friends before acting for himself. Hence Darcy's reluctance to become involved with the Bennett family, whose low breeding would affect his own social standing. Hence also the terrible shame that Lydia's elopement, if it had not been legalized by marriage, would have brought to the whole family. The chances of the other daughters marrying after such a scandal would have been greatly reduced.

Appearance   In a society which imposes a strict code of social behaviour, where a certain 'performance' is expected in public, where a certain degree of hypocrisy is necessary, appearance and reality can often be confused. This problem comes to light chiefly in the characters of Darcy and Wickham. The former, because he fails to behave as society expects, is censured and his name is blackened. The latter, because he is sociable and genial, is generally agreed to be of better character. Once the prejudice sets in it is difficult to remove. Other characters, too, deceive and are deceived. Miss Bingley appears to be all that was expected of a lady. Elizabeth sees beneath her façade to the jealousy, spite and snobbery that lie behind. Darcy is taken in by Jane's appearance, leading him to believe that she has no strong feelings for Bingley. Jane Austen warns of the necessity of judging people properly before forming an opinion of them.

Etiquette Within the society that Jane Austen describes there is a strict etiquette which has to be observed. One such rule is the correct procedure for introduction. Mrs Bennet begs her husband to go and visit Mr Bingley, their new neighbour, otherwise she and her daughters will not be able to visit. In the same way it is expected of Mr Bingley that he must return a visit to the Bennets, if he is to be thought courteous. Elizabeth feels that Mr Collins will breach etiquette if he introduces himself to Mr Darcy, for the latter is 'superior in consequence'. Mr Collins ignores her advice but is treated with 'an air of distant civility' for having broken the code. Darcy himself, though, is accused of discourteous behaviour when he refuses to dance even though there was an obvious shortage of men.

Manners There is a strong emphasis placed on manners in this society. The word Jane Austen uses most frequently to sum up the expected mode of behaviour is 'civility'. Even when affronted, the well-bred person will respond with 'cold civility'. Certain unwritten rules of conduct determine whether a person is well-bred or not. Miss Bingley suggests that a lady should 'possess a certain something . . . in her tone of voice, her address and her expressions'. Elizabeth, always conscious of the way she speaks and careful of the words she chooses, is aware of the offence that thoughtless language can give. Her mother, and other members of the family, are, however, not so far-sighted. Their behaviour at the Netherfield Ball is a fine example of bad manners and ill-breeding and it leaves Elizabeth cringing with embarrassment.

Maybe Mrs Bennet, who is not from such a highborn family, can be excused her social *faux pas*, but Caroline Bingley and Lady de Bourgh should know better. Both reveal bad manners towards Elizabeth, the former by being spiteful, the latter by being insulting. The importance attached to breeding can not be better illustrated than by the way Darcy was seriously put off Elizabeth because of her family's bad manners.

Structure

Jane Austen is renowned for the skill with which she constructs her novel. No aspect of character, no detail of plot, no word of language is wasted. All fit together to make a unified work.

Pride and Prejudice can be seen as two similar halves meeting in the middle with the climax of Darcy's proposal. The novel begins with Bingley's and Darcy's arrival at Netherfield and ends with their return to Netherfield. The first half sees the build up of pride and prejudice between Elizabeth and Darcy; the second half shows it breaking down. Each half includes a sudden marriage, each a journey for Elizabeth, both of which end in a surprise for her. Lady de Bourgh has two arguments with Elizabeth, one near the end of the first half, one near the end of the second.

Jane Austen cleverly prepares the reader for each event in the novel so nothing is really a surprise for the thoughtful reader. Bingley's character was seen to be compliant so his sudden departure is no real surprise. We are aware of Charlotte's views on marriage so her acceptance of Mr Collins is not unexpected. Even Darcy's proposal is prepared for by his frequent visits and growth of interest in Elizabeth. Lydia's elopement is predicted by a thorough knowledge of her character and the recent news of Wickham's previous infamous behaviour with Darcy's sister.

Jane Austen makes great use of contrast in describing her characters. Her two main pairs of characters are portrayed as opposites. Darcy, reserved and haughty, is compared with Bingley who is agreeable and at ease in society. Elizabeth, sceptical and perceptive, is set against Jane, who is naïve and accepting. Mr Bennet's intelligence is contrasted with Mrs Bennet's stupidity. Darcy's 'forbidding disagreeable' countenance is contrasted with Wickham's 'amiable' countenance. The greatest difference of all is, of course, the contrast in temperament between Elizabeth and Darcy. The former is lively and teasing, the latter serious. Thus character is highlighted and exposed by the use of this device.

The novel includes forty-four letters ranging from mere invitations to the most crucial one of all, that in which Mr Darcy explains himself after Elizabeth has rejected his proposal. The letter performs two main functions. Firstly it plays a large part in the construction of the plot. The most obvious example is, again, Darcy's letter. It causes the beginning of Elizabeth's change of heart, an essential requirement for the successful completion of the novel. Also signficant to the plot are Jane's letters to Elizabeth in Derbyshire telling of the elopement (note the clever way the information is split between two letters to create dramatic tension), and Mrs Gardiner's letter to Elizabeth revealing Mr Darcy's part in Wickham's salvation.

The letter's other function is to reveal character. Mr Collins's letter heralding his arrival reveals his character exactly. His letters after Lydia's elopement and their marriage reveal an odious display of self-centredness and hypocrisy. Darcy's letter to Elizabeth after the proposal reveals the beginnings of a change in his character. Lydia's letters show the irresponsibility and selfishness of her character.

Love and marriage

Although this book is chiefly concerned with marriage Jane Austen does not often use the word love. When she does she is sceptical of its meaning. The phrase 'violently in love' she describes as 'hackneyed, doubtful and indefinite'. To her it can mean anything from a short acquaintance to a 'strong attachment'. She is uncertain of the lasting qualities of passionate love, convinced that it is not a strong enough basis for marriage. True love is rational as well as emotional. It is based on mutual esteem, respect and gratitude and it arises from a clearsighted understanding of the other person. Passion is part of it, but it is controlled, True love has the power to change people. Elizabeth attributes Darcy's loss of pride to 'love, ardent love'. It has the power to persuade people. Conscious of Darcy's regard for her, Elizabeth grows to love him partly through gratitude for his love.

Jane Austen is interested in the way people select their partner and the main theme of the novel is marriage. In a book that includes four weddings there is plenty of scope to explore this theme. She describes three different kinds of marriage. There is the mercenary marriage brought about entirely for economic reasons. The union between Mr Collins and Charlotte Lucas is a good example of this. Charlotte is pessimistic about finding happiness in marriage anyway, and believes she may as well marry for security. For someone without personal fortune, this was obviously an attractive reason.

Almost completely in contrast to this prudent view is the marriage that is based solely on passion and physical attraction. Lydia and Wickham made such a marriage as did Mr and Mrs Bennet, years before. The success of such a union can be judged by looking at the relationship between Mr and Mrs Bennet. Once the excitement of 'youth and beauty' had faded the two people found that they did not understand, or even like each other.

Somewhere in between these two views of marriage lies the ideal state. It is seen in the relationships between Elizabeth and Darcy, Jane and Bingley. Both relationships are 'rationally founded', based on an 'excellent understanding' and a 'general similarity of feeling and taste'. Jane Austen, true to 18th-century classical tradition, places a firm belief in reason dominating emotion. She acknowledges that both partners must have a compatibility of interests, temperament and intelligence for a marriage to work well.

Jane Austen lived in a mercenary world. The income and property of the local gentry are openly discussed. No secret is made of the need to marry for money. A woman who has no fortune must look for a man who has, and vice versa, something which even Elizabeth admits. She criticizes Charlotte, not for marrying a wealthy man, but for marrying solely for money. She quite accepts Wickham's motives for changing his interest to a Miss King, a rich woman. Mrs Bennet's fixation with marriage can largely be explained by the poor financial position of her daughters. Nevertheless, Jane Austen would be the last to deny the important part that money plays. If it had not been for the generosity of Darcy settling a large sum of money on Wickham none of the Bennet girls would have stood much chance of marrying.

Prejudice

Although the book is concerned chiefly with Elizabeth's prejudice against Darcy, she is not the only one who experiences this feeling. Elizabeth takes an immediate dislike to Mr Darcy because of his supercilious attitude, and also because he hurts her pride with his unkind remarks. Prejudiced against Darcy, she is easily deceived by Wickham because she wants to believe badly of Darcy. It is interesting to see how differently she looks upon Darcy before and after she discovers the truth about his character. Before receiving the letter which changes everything, she can see no further than 'his pride, his abominable pride'. At Pemberley, after the revelations of his letter, she is 'amazed at the alteration in his manner', an alteration partially due to his loss of pride, but also to her loss of prejudice. Darcy, in his own way, is also prejudiced. He fights his attraction to Elizabeth because of the prejudice he feels towards her ill-bred family.

Pride

One of the subjects under question in the book is obviously the nature of pride. Darcy is severely censured for his pride by Elizabeth and public opinion in general. It is deserved, as his uncivil behaviour at Netherfield offended the etiquette of the time, although Charlotte thought his social rank gave him the right to haughty manners. Darcy himself attributed his lack of ease to shyness, not pride. Even if that were true, Elizabeth believed that that was no defence as shyness could be overcome with 'practice'. Darcy does admit to being wrongly proud over the question of rank. He thought that it mattered greatly that Elizabeth's family was socially inferior but he does finally see that it is of secondary importance compared with winning the girl he loves. Elizabeth, too, is guilty of pride. In fact it is arguable that her prejudice against Darcy arose primarily from hurt pride.

Analysis chart

Dates
The story unfolds over a twelve-month period – often thought to be in 1811 and 1812. However, there is a sense of timelessness about the novel which makes the actual years unimportant.

	1	2	3	4	5	6	7	8	9	10	11	12	13	14	15	16	17	18	19	20	21	22	23	24	25	26
Dates	29 September		October				13 November						18 November					26 November	27 November							
Chapter	1	2	3	4	5	6	7	8	9	10	11	12	13	14	15	16	17	18	19	20	21	22	23	24	25	26

Important events
- Ch 1: News of Mr Bingley
- Ch 3: Assembly Ball at Meryton
- Ch 6: At the Lucases – first meeting of Elizabeth & Darcy
- Ch 7: Jane & Elizabeth at Netherfield
- Ch 13: Mr Collins arrives at Longbourn
- Ch 16: Mr Wickham talks about Mr Darcy
- Ch 18: The ball at Netherfield
- Ch 19: Mr Collins proposes to Elizabeth
- Ch 21: The Netherfield party departs
- Ch 22: Mr Collins proposes to Charlotte – successfully
- Ch 24: The Gardiners arrive
- Ch 25: Charlotte & Mr Collins married. Gardiners & Jane to London

	1	2	3	4	5	6	7	8	9	10	11	12	13	14	15	16	17	18	19	20	21	22	23	24	25	26
Places Longbourn	●	●	●	●	●	●	●	●				●	●	●	●	●	●		●	●	●	●	●	●	●	●
Netherfield			●			●	●	●	●	●	●	●						●								
London																										●
Hunsford & Rosings																										
Pemberley & Lambton																										
Characters Elizabeth	●		●	●		●	●	●	●	●	●					●	●	●	●			●	●		●	●
Mr Darcy			●		●	●		●	●	●	●						●	●	●						●	
Jane				●		●												●				●			●	●
Mr Bingley			●	●				●	●	●											●					
Lydia		●					●			●			●											●		
Mr Wickham															●	●	●	●								
Charlotte						●	●											●					●			
Mr Collins													●	●	●	●	●	●	●							●
Mr & Mrs Bennet	●	●	●			●			●				●	●	●			●		●			●	●		
The Gardiners																									●	
Lady Catherine														●		●			●							
Aspects Aspects of Language	●	●	●	●	●	●	●	●	●	●	●					●	●	●				●	●			
Social aspects	●	●	●	●	●	●	●	●	●	●				●		●	●	●							●	
Structure						●	●	●		●								●				●			●	●
Love & marriage	●					●	●			●				●				●			●	●	●		●	●
Prejudice			●							●	●							●							●	●
Pride			●			●	●			●								●				●				
Page in commentary on which chapter first appears	19	20	20	21	22	22	24	25	26	27	29	—	30	30	31	33	34	35	36	36	36	36	37	37	38	38

Ch.	Time	Event
27	March	Elizabeth in London
28		Elizabeth visits Charlotte
29		
30		
31	Easter Day	Mr Darcy visits Elizabeth at the Parsonage
32		Col Fitzwilliam talks to Mr Darcy
33		
34		Mr Darcy proposes to Elizabeth
35		Mr Darcy's letter to Elizabeth
36		
37		
38		Elizabeth leaves Hunsford
39	2nd week in May	
40		Elizabeth meets Wickham again
41	Last week in May	Lydia goes to Brighton
42	June/July	
43		Elizabeth at Pemberley
44		
45		
46		News of Lydia's elopement
47		Lydia's letter
48		Letter from Mr Collins
49	1st week in August	News of Lydia & Mr Wickham
50		
51		Lydia & Mr Wickham married and return to Longbourn
52		The letter from Mrs Gardiner
53	2nd week in September	Mr Darcy & Mr Bingley visit Longbourn
54		
55		Mr Bingley proposes to Jane
56		Lady Catherine visits Elizabeth
57		Letter from Mr Collins about Mr Darcy & Elizabeth
58		Elizabeth & Mr Darcy declare their love
59		Elizabeth & Mr Darcy formally engaged
60		
61		

Bottom row: 39 39 40 41 41 42 43 43 44 44 46 46 46 47 47 48 48 50 50 50 51 51 52 53 53 54 54 55 55 56 57 57 58 — —

Finding your way around the commentary

Each page of the commentary gives the following information:

1 A quotation from the start of each paragraph on which a comment is made, or act/scene or line numbers plus a quotation, so that you can easily locate the right place in your text.

2 A series of comments, explaining, interpreting, and drawing your attention to important incidents, characters and aspects of the text.

3 For each comment, headings to indicate the important characters, themes, and ideas dealt with in the comment.

4 For each heading, a note of the comment numbers in this guide where the previous or next comment dealing with that heading occurred.

Thus you can use this commentary section in a number of ways.

1 Turn to that part of the commentary dealing with the chapter/act you are perhaps revising for a class discussion or essay. Read through the comments in sequence, referring all the time to the text, which you should have open before you. The comments will direct your attention to all the important things of which you should take note.

2 Take a single character or topic from the list on page 17. Note the comment number next to it. Turn to that comment in this guide, where you will find the first of a number of comments on your chosen topic. Study it, and the appropriate part of your text to which it will direct you. Note the comment number in this guide where the next comment for your topic occurs and turn to it when you are ready. Thus, you can follow one topic right through your text. If you have an essay to write on a particular character or theme just follow the path through this guide and you will soon find everything you need to know!

3 A number of relevant relationships between characters and topics are listed on page 17. To follow these relationships throughout your text, turn to the comment indicated. As the previous and next comment are printed at the side of each page in the commentary, it is a simple matter to flick through the pages to find the previous or next occurrence of the relationship in which you are interested.

For example, you want to examine in depth the social aspects of the novel. Turning to the single topic list, you will find that 'Social aspects' first occurs in comment 3. On turning to comment 3 you will discover a zero (0) in the place of the previous reference (because this is the first time that it has occurred) and the number 13 for the next reference. You now turn to comment 13 and find that the previous comment number is 3 (from where you have just been looking) and that the next reference is to comment 14, and so on throughout the text.

You also wish to trace the relationship between Elizabeth and Darcy throughout the novel. From the relationships list, you are directed to comment 34. This is the first time that both Elizabeth and Darcy are discussed together and you will find that the next time that this happens occurs in comment 35 (the 'next' reference for both Elizabeth and Darcy). On to comment 35 and you will now discover that two different comment numbers are given for the subject under examination – numbers 45 and 36. This is because each character is traced separately as well as together and you will have to continue tracing them separately until you finally come to comment 72 – the next occasion on which both Elizabeth and Darcy are discussed.

Previous appearance in guide

Quote from novel

Character or idea under discussion

Comment number

6 'Mr Bennet how can . . .'
In studying the theme of marriage Jane Austen gives examples of good and bad marriages. Looking at the sarcastic way Mr Bennet answers his wife, into what category do you think their marriage falls? Make sure you can give reasons for your choice.

4/7   Mr and Mrs Bennett
1/7   Love and marriage

Next appearance in guide

Commentary

Single topics:

	Comment no:		Comment no:
Aspects of language	1	Lydia	12
Social aspects	3	Mr Wickham	94
Structure	30	Mr and Mrs Bennet	2
Love and marriage	1	Lady Catherine	87
Prejudice	18	The Gardiners	149
Pride	19	The Lucases	27
Elizabeth	5	Miss Bingley	23
Mr Darcy	17	Fitzwilliam	173
Jane	21	Kitty and Mary	10
Mr Bingley	16		
Charlotte	29		
Mr Collins	84		

Relationships:

			Comment no:
Elizabeth	and	Mr Darcy	34
Elizabeth	and	Prejudice	71
Elizabeth	and	Pride	38
Mr Darcy	and	Prejudice	18
Mr Darcy	and	Pride	19
Jane	and	Mr Bingley	277
Love and marriage	and	Elizabeth	31
Love and marriage	and	Jane	281
Love and marriage	and	Charlotte	31
Love and marriage	and	Mr and Mrs Bennet	6
Love and marriage	and	Mr Collins	86
Love and marriage	and	Mr Darcy	239

Commentary

Chapter 1

1 It is a truth . . .
In the opening sentence Jane Austen sums up the theme of her book. She is being ironic, implying that very often it is the parents with daughters who are hunting the single men of 'good fortune'.

2 'Do not you . . .'
Jane Austen uses dialogue very effectively to reveal character. Look at the way Mr Bennet teases his wife; he must know why Mr Bingley's arrival is of great importance yet he pretends not to. What does this reveal about Mr Bennet's attitude to his wife's preoccupations?

3 'But consider your . . .'
Notice the strict code of behaviour at this time. It would have seemed discourteous for the women to visit without previous formal introduction by the head of the household.

4 'You are over . . .'
Again notice the difference in attitude. For Mrs Bennet the business of meeting all eligible bachelors is very serious. Mr Bennet can only make light of it. He mocks her seriousness and teases her again. How does Mrs Bennet react to his mockery? What does this tell you about her character? Look at the end of this chapter to see how Jane Austen describes her.

5 'They have none . . .'
Although we have not met her yet we can expect, from what her father says, that she has a special quality of intelligence and wit that her sisters lack.

6 'Mr Bennet how can . . .'
In studying the theme of marriage Jane Austen gives examples of good and bad marriages. Looking at the sarcastic way Mr Bennet answers his wife, into what category do you think their marriage falls? Make sure you can give reasons for your choice.

7 Mr Bennet was so . . .
The characters of Mr and Mrs Bennet are summed up in this last paragraph. How close could their marriage have been, if twenty-three years has been 'insufficient to make his wife understand his character'? Try to think why this lack of understanding exists and the parts played in that lack, by both Mr and Mrs Bennet.

Characters and ideas
previous/next comment

0/6	Love and marriage
0/2	Aspects of language
0/4	Mr and Mrs Bennet
1/9	Aspects of language
0/13	Social aspects
2/6	Mr and Mrs Bennet
0/20	Elizabeth
4/7	Mr and Mrs Bennet
1/7	Love and marriage
6/8	Mr and Mrs Bennet
6/31	Love and marriage

Chapter 2

8 Mrs Bennet deigned . . .
Notice how irritable she becomes because she thinks her plans are frustrated by her husband's refusal to pay a call on Bingley.

9 'Kitty has no . . .'
Mr Bennet is very sarcastic about Kitty and Mary on the next page. He is also mocking his wife, by using the kind of arguments that she would normally use herself. Why do you think he kept his introduction a secret? What do you think his constant need to tease reveals about his state of mind?

10 'What can be the . . .'
The most serious of the five Bennet girls, Mary tries to derive wisdom from the reading of books. Unlike her father and sister Elizabeth, she lacks the perception to judge people by their behaviour alone, so her pronouncements, when she does make them, sound empty and irrelevant. Look at the end of chapter 5, and chapter 47 – the conversation in the dining-room.

11 'How good it was . . .'
Notice her complete change of mood on hearing this good news. This is a good example of her 'uncertain temper' as described by Jane Austen at the end of the last chapter.

12 'Oh!' said Lydia . . .
Notice how we are immediately made aware of Lydia's self-confidence.

13 The rest of the . . .
Notice the assumption of a set pattern of social behaviour. Mr Bingley must visit the Bennets because Mr Bennet visited him.

Chapter 3

14 Not all that . . .
Jane Austen mocks the general assumptions of public opinion in the sentence 'To be fond of dancing . . .'. Yet there is truth in this statement. Very often, the dance was one of the only ways that two people could have a private conversation in public. Look at chapter 18 to see how Elizabeth and Darcy make use of this social convention.

15 'If I can but . . .'
The aim of Mrs Bennet's life is summarized in this sentence.

16 Mr Bingley was good . . .
The general opinion of Mr Bingley's appearance and manner agrees with Mr Lucas's impression on the previous page. Notice how the newcomers are described through the eyes of all the people present. Jane Austen is emphasizing the importance, in their society, of the individual being a part of a larger group, answerable to others as much as to himself.

Characters and ideas	
previous/next comment	
7/9	Mr and Mrs Bennet
8/11	Mr and Mrs Bennet
2/14	Aspects of language
0/36	Kitty and Mary
9/15	Mr and Mrs Bennet
0/44	Lydia
3/14	Social aspects
13/16	Social aspects
9/25	Aspects of language
11/43	Mr and Mrs Bennet
0/26	Mr Bingley
14/17	Social aspects

17 Mr Bingley was good . . .
Jane Austen again satirizes public opinion. The rumour of Mr Darcy's wealth is taken as fact, and he is judged by all by his appearance, 'his forbidding, disagreeable countenance'.

0/18	Mr Darcy
16/21	Social aspects

18 Mr Bingley had soon . . .
The general opinion is quickly formed about Mr Darcy. 'His character was decided' on the strength of his unsociable behaviour. Heightened by the contrast with Bingley's amiable behaviour, his proud behaviour is condemned by all. Prejudice against him sets in.

17/19	Mr Darcy
0/71	Prejudice

19 'Come, Darcy,' said . . .
The dialogue forcefully reveals Darcy's pride. Later he maintains it was shyness that led to his awkward behaviour at the ball. Do you think, though, that his comments, especially about Elizabeth, can be excused in such a way? Has not Elizabeth real grounds for prejudice after that?

18/26	Mr Darcy
0/28	Pride

20 Mr Bingley followed . . .
Notice Elizabeth's reaction to Darcy's insult. What does it say about her character that she is able to laugh it off? Look how her behaviour here is confirmed by her own words in chapter 11 when she says 'I hope I never ridicule . . .'.

5/21	Elizabeth

Chapter 4

21 When Jane and Elizabeth . . .
As if to illustrate the point made later on the page, Jane is shown to accept people at face value. She is impressed with Bingley because of his good breeding and manners. Elizabeth is mocking her a little when she says, 'His character is thereby complete'. Elizabeth feels one's judgment must be more discerning than that and yet it is she, not Jane, who is guilty later of being deceived by appearances.

20/23	Elizabeth
0/23	Jane
17/22	Social aspects

22 'He is just . . .'
Manners and breeding were of considerable importance in upper class circles. They play a major role in the book as it is the Bennet family's lack of breeding that is a major impediment in the course of the relationship between Elizabeth and Darcy.

21/24	Social aspects

23 'Oh! you are . . .'
In this dialogue Elizabeth draws attention to Jane's kind nature: 'All the world are . . .'. How does Jane's ability to see good in everyone affect her judgment? Look at what she says about the Bingley sisters on the next page. Does Elizabeth share her view that Miss Bingley is 'charming'? As we get to know Miss Bingley better, think about whether Elizabeth's 'quickness of observation' has led her to a truer assessment of her character.

0/24	Miss Bingley
21/30	Jane
21/31	Elizabeth

24 Elizabeth listened . . .
To belong to a family whose fortune was made in trade was to belong to an inferior class. Jane Austen is gently mocking the Bingley sisters' desire to

23/25	Miss Bingley
22/25	Social aspects

Characters and ideas previous/next comment

forget their origins. It is particularly ironic when we see Miss Bingley's lack of respect for the Bennet family because they have relations in 'trade'.

25 Elizabeth listened . . .
Miss Bingley and her sister had every right to be called 'ladies' as they fulfilled all the requirements. They have money, beauty and a good education. Jane Austen is being ironic when she says that they are 'entitled to think well of themselves . . .' as their subsequent behaviour, particularly in regard to the Bennets, is far from 'ladylike'.

26 Between him and . . .
The two men are described as being quite opposite in temperament. Bingley is easy-going and sociable; Darcy is complicated and distant. Of the two, Darcy is the more intelligent and Bingley admires his judgement. To illustrate this contrast their impressions of the ball are totally opposed.

Chapter 5

27 Within a short . . .
Jane Austen uses satire to describe Sir William Lucas's new position as a gentleman. In a society clearly divided by rank, he regards it as important to loosen all connection with a past life. Although Elizabeth mocks him gently, he is not an unpleasant character.

28 'Miss Bingley told . . .'
It is left to Jane to find something good to say about Darcy. She is the only one to suggest that his reserve is due more to shyness than pride.

29 'His pride,' said . . .
Do you agree with Miss Lucas that Darcy's rank justifies his pride? What does her tolerance of Darcy's character tell you about Miss Lucas's attitude to men of fortune? How does this remark prepare us for future events?

Chapter 6

30 'It may perhaps . . .'
Charlotte's remark that Jane 'may lose the opportunity of fixing' Bingley because of her 'composure of temper and uniform cheerfulness', is proved correct later in the novel. Look at Darcy's letter in chapter 35, to see that this is exactly the reason Darcy gives for believing that Jane had no special affection for Bingley. This is an excellent example of the care Jane Austen has taken to construct a plot in which all comments are significant and every character has an intrinsic role.

31 'Perhaps he must, . . .'
Charlotte's views on marriage are obviously distinctly different from Elizabeth's. Charlotte is concerned chiefly with obtaining a good financial

	Characters and ideas
	previous/next comment

match; sentiment can follow later. She is quite prepared to scheme in order to get a man. Elizabeth feels that marriage is most importantly a union based on mutual knowledge and understanding. She protests that Jane does not know Bingley well enough to have decided whether or not she is in love.

	7/32	Love and marriage

32 'Well,' said Charlotte . . .
Charlotte makes it clear that she sees marriage primarily as an economic matter. Her expectations are no higher than that. Again note the clever way that Jane Austen prepares us for future events. Knowing her views it is not surprising when Charlotte accepts Mr Collins's proposal.

	31/115	Charlotte
	31/43	Love and marriage
	30/44	Structure

33 'You make me laugh, . . .'
Elizabeth rejects Charlotte's cynical view of marriage. Notice the dramatic irony in her comment, 'You would never act in this way yourself'!

	31/34	Elizabeth
	27/35	Aspects of language

34 'Occupied in observing . . .'
Darcy, still acknowledging that Elizabeth's manners are 'not those of the fashionable world', is nevertheless attracted by her 'playfulness'. Unbeknown to her his interest in her is increasing.

	29/35	Mr Darcy
	33/35	Elizabeth
	27/37	Social aspects

35 'What does Mr Darcy . . .'
As if she understood what Darcy was thinking, Elizabeth proceeds to reveal the 'playfulness' of her character in the ensuing dialogue. She is lively and teasing towards him and determined to use the weapon of her wit to face his 'satirical eye'.

	34/39	Mr Darcy
	34/36	Elizabeth
	33/45	Aspects of language

36 Her performance was . . .
Mary is not a very attractive character. Set against Elizabeth her failings seem more intense. She has neither 'genius nor taste'. Her pedantic air and conceited manner contrast poorly with Elizabeth's 'easy and unaffected' character.

	35/38	Elizabeth
	10/44	Kitty and Mary

37 'What a charming . . .'
Sir William, although genial, is pompous. Conscious of his new-found rank, he wants it to be known and recognized by men of society like Darcy. Like the other pompous character in the book, Mr Collins, he is not aware when he is being patronized, and allows Darcy to make impolite remarks at his expense.

	27/136	The Lucases
	34/40	Social aspects

38 'Indeed, Sir, I have . . .'
Elizabeth, too, has her pride. Look at the reasons why she refuses to dance with Darcy.

	36/39	Elizabeth
	29/72	Pride

39 Elizabeth looked archly . . .
Why do you think Elizabeth has not 'injured' herself with Darcy by refusing to dance with him? What quality of character do you think he sees behind this refusal?

	35/41	Mr Darcy
	38/47	Elizabeth

40 'You are considering . . .'
Caroline Bingley expresses contempt at the dullness of present society. These people talk of nothing yet create much noise. How do the previous conversations between Sir William and Darcy, and the musical recital justify her complaint?

37/42   Social aspects

41 'Your conjecture is . . .'
Why do you think Darcy has changed his opinion of Elizabeth? Before she was merely 'tolerable', now she has 'a pair of fine eyes' and is 'pretty'.

39/42   Mr Darcy

42 'Miss Elizabeth Bennet!' . . .
As sneering of the present company as Elizabeth first imagined, Caroline Bingley is surprised by Darcy's contradiction. The jealousy she feels forces her to be sarcastic when she asks 'pray when am I to wish you joy?' Yet she brings up an important issue when she mentions Mrs Bennet shortly after. Although Darcy does not show it, he is concerned about Mrs Bennet's lack of social grace.

41/51   Mr Darcy
25/48   Miss Bingley
40/47   Social aspects

Chapter 7

43 Mr Bennet's property . . .
The information about the 'entailment' of the estate is important as it explains Mrs Bennet's near obsession with the subject of marriage. Her concern is mainly economic. Because none of them will inherit their father's estate they will not be able to keep themselves in the manner accustomed, unless they marry well.

15/44   Mr and Mrs
         Bennet
32/73   Love and
         marriage

44 'From all that . . .'
The two girls seem very impressed with superficialities such as the 'regimentals of an ensign', thus proving the observation near the beginning of this chapter that 'their minds were more vacant than their sisters' '. Their father is contemptuous of their chatter but their attitude to him differs, one from the other. It is significant that while Catherine takes heed, Lydia totally ignores him. Again the cleverness of the structure of the novel is noticeable. Lydia's and Catherine's future actions are totally in keeping with their characters.

36/90   Kitty and Mary
43/45   Mr and Mrs
         Bennet
12/64   Lydia
32/51   Structure

45 'If my children . . .'
Mr Bennet is being totally ironic in his conversation with his wife. In almost no respect do they agree and again he is having fun at her expense. Her lack of perception is evident in the way she defends all her daughters, regardless of their actions. Her remark 'When they get to our age . . .' is quite foolish and, in a way, untrue. She does think about officers, as possible husbands for her daughters!

44/46   Mr and Mrs
         Bennet
35/48   Aspects of
         language

46 'No, my dear . . .'
Despite her lack of intelligence she has enough guile to formulate a scheme that would keep Jane at Netherfield over night. However, her foolishness surfaces when she smugly praises herself for the success of the idea,

45/57   Mr and Mrs
         Bennet

showing no regard for her daughter's well-being in the rain, and dismissing out of hand Mr Bennet's comment a few paragraphs on – 'if she should die, it would be . . .'.

47 Elizabeth, feeling really . . .
Her independence of spirit is again shown by her decision to make the walk to Netherfield alone. The effect of the walk on her complexion is not lost on Darcy as we see on the next page, although the Bingley sisters are horrified at such unorthodox behaviour.

39/49	Elizabeth
42/48	Social aspects

Chapter 8

48 Their brother, indeed, . . .
Jane Austen satirically describes the people of so-called 'superior' birth. Mr Hurst, who she previously says 'merely looked the gentleman' is described as an 'indolent' man of few interests. Miss Bingley, for all her superior education and fortune behaves in an ill-bred manner, criticizing Elizabeth in her absence. Her comment on the next page about Elizabeth's lack of 'decorum' shows what a hypocrite she is.

42/49	Miss Bingley
47/51	Social aspects
45/50	Aspects of language

49 When dinner was over . . .
What drives Miss Bingley to be so critical of Elizabeth? – Look back at the commentary on chapter 6: 'Miss Elizabeth Bennet!'.

48/50	Miss Bingley
47/54	Elizabeth

50 'I have an excessive . . .'
Note the use of the word 'sweet' to describe Jane. It reflects her patronizing attitude to Jane. The same note of condescension is ironically picked up by Jane Austen a few lines further on in the use of the word 'dear'.

49/54	Miss Bingley
48/55	Aspects of language

51 'I have an excessive . . .'
Notice the importance attached to the status of all members of the family when choosing a partner for marriage. Notice too how different Bingley's and Darcy's views are on the subject. What do Bingley's tell you about his feelings for Jane already? How does Darcy's comment prepare us for later events in the book?

26/52	Mr Bingley
42/55	Mr Darcy
44/68	Structure
48/53	Social aspects

52 'In nursing your . . .'
Bingley's kind nature is seen here in contrast to his sister's spiteful character. Here and just previously he tries to reduce the sharpness of Miss Bingley's retorts with sympathetic remarks.

51/58	Mr Bingley

53 'Oh! certainly,' . . .
This rather idealized picture of the 'accomplished' woman gives an insight into the kinds of activities upper class women took part in during Jane Austen's time. Theirs was a gentle, delicate existence which did not include robust physical exertion. Look back to near the end of chapter 7, for the criticism that Elizabeth received for walking (through mud!) to Netherfield. This was just not ladylike!

51/56	Social aspects

54 'I am no longer . . .'
Notice Elizabeth's independence of mind and her down-to-earth nature. Caroline Bingley, in an attempt to impress Darcy, agrees with him to an absurd extreme in their discussion of a woman's accomplishments. Elizabeth's comment, 'I am no longer . . .' reveals her own superior intelligence and wit.

50/55	Miss Bingley
49/62	Elizabeth

55 'Undoubtedly,' replied . . .
Notice the beautiful irony in Darcy's reply. What 'arts' has Miss Bingley been using to 'captivate' Darcy? Reread the previous page to see how she tries to flatter Darcy. How do you know that Darcy has seen through her ploy?

54/66	Miss Bingley
51/59	Mr Darcy
50/58	Aspects of language

Chapter 9

56 'You may depend . . .'
The oil that lubricated the social intercourse of this class of people was 'civility'. Even Miss Bingley who had no respect whatsoever for Mrs Bennet managed to speak to her with 'cold' civility. Look back to the middle of chapter 3 and examine the way Darcy spoke of Elizabeth on first seeing her. That is why he was so severely censured by public opinion; he lacked 'civility'.

53/57	Social aspects

57 'I am sure,' she . . .
The lack of breeding in Mrs Bennet's character is apparent in the scene when she quizzes Bingley on his intentions to leave or stay at Netherfield. On the next page she reveals her hostility towards Darcy and makes herself look foolish by misunderstanding his comment about country people. Elizabeth 'blushing for her mother' tries to change the subject.

46/60	Mr and Mrs Bennet
56/59	Social aspects

58 'Whatever I do . . .'
Notice the dramatic irony here. What in fact does Bingley do, on Darcy's instigation? Look forward to the first paragraph of chapter 24, for the answer.

52/63	Mr Bingley
55/62	Aspects of language

59 'The country,' said . . .
There is an underlying assumption that country life and therefore country people are dull. Look back at Darcy's boredom with the evening's entertainment, in the middle of chapter 6, and Miss Bingley's comments near the end of that chapter. This prejudice against country people explains his comment in chapter 32, that Elizabeth 'cannot have been always at Longbourn'.

55/60	Mr Darcy
57/61	Social aspects

60 'Certainly, my dear, . . .'
As if to confirm Darcy's feelings about the narrowness of country life, Mrs Bennet boasts in a childish, unintelligent way about the number of families they socialize with.

57/61	Mr and Mrs Bennet
59/61	Mr Darcy

61 'Yes, she called . . .'
To whom is Mrs Bennet referring when she talks about 'those persons who fancy themselves . . .'? Look at the comments under 'Social aspects' in chapters 4, 8, 31, and elsewhere in this guide. Is her definition of breeding correct? Is Darcy's behaviour at the ball an example of good breeding? Could you at this stage define a 'well-bred person'?

60/83	Mr and Mrs Bennet
60/62	Mr Darcy
59/73	Social aspects

62 Darcy only smiled; . . .
Darcy cannot help but be impressed with Elizabeth's wit. She is forced to try and lighten the situation, for her mother's boasting and tactless conversation is creating an awkward atmosphere.

61/65	Mr Darcy
54/69	Elizabeth
58/76	Aspects of language

63 Darcy only smiled . . .
What does Bingley think of Mrs Bennet's behaviour? Look back a few paragraphs – 'Yes, indeed . . .' to gain an impression of his easy-going character in the face of such an embarrassment.

58/67	Mr Bingley

64 'Lydia was a stout, . . .'
Is it surprising that she is a 'favourite with her mother'? In answering this you might like to consider their two characters. Are they alike in character? What do you think of her question to Mr Bingley? Is it misplaced? Take into account not only the conventions of this society, but also the whole tone of this conversation and Mr Bingley's reply.

44/90	Lydia

65 'Mrs Bennet and her . . .'
How far does the final sentence of the chapter indicate his change of heart towards Elizabeth?

62/66	Mr Darcy

Chapter 10

66 'Will you give me . . .'
Miss Bingley, in her attempt to ingratiate herself with Mr Darcy, is merely making herself look foolish, and becoming the butt of his sarcasm.

55/74	Miss Bingley
65/67	Mr Darcy

67 'That will not . . .'
Letters form an important part of the novel. One of their chief uses is to reveal character. The contrast between Darcy and Bingley is again emphasized by the description of their different styles of writing. In what way does Darcy's considered style of writing reveal his character? How is Bingley's more careless style in keeping with his own character? Can you give examples from their actions and conversations to support your views?

63/68	Mr Bingley
66/69	Mr Darcy

68 'You expect me . . .'
Darcy and Bingley discuss the pliancy of Bingley's character. Again, notice the carefully thought out structure of the book. Jane Austen is preparing us for Bingley's subsequent, rapid departure.

67/70	Mr Bingley
51/84	Structure

Characters and ideas previous/next comment

69 'By all means, . . .'
To bring the argument to a close, for it has become drawn out, Bingley teases Darcy and makes light of the whole discussion. Note Darcy's reaction: he is not amused. This inability to laugh at himself is a failing that Elizabeth notices here and later on near the end of chapter 58.

67/72	Mr Darcy
62/71	Elizabeth

70 'Perhaps I do. . . .'
Bingley's easy-going nature finds arguments unpleasant. He does not share Darcy's and Elizabeth's pleasure in witty repartee.

68/135	Mr Bingley

71 Mrs Hurst sang . . .
Notice how Elizabeth's prejudice blinds her to Darcy's true feelings. She is unaware that his interest in her is based on a growing admiration for her. She mistakenly believes he disapproves of her. She does not care for she still dislikes him, 'She liked him too little . . .'.

69/72	Elizabeth
18/82	Prejudice

72 'Do not you . . .'
A reel was a country dance. Elizabeth's interpretation of Mr Darcy's request was that he wished to insult her by inferring that she, a 'country bumpkin' would enjoy dancing a reel. Her pride is hurt. How do you interpret his capitulating reply?

69/74	Mr Darcy
71/75	Elizabeth
38/105	Pride

73 Elizabeth, having . . .
Note that although Darcy is falling in love with Elizabeth, her family still prevent him from believing that there is any future in it.

43/86	Love and marriage
61/75	Social aspects

74 She often tried . . .
It is when Miss Bingley is most jealous that her behaviour becomes most odious. Having understood Darcy's deep reservations about the Bennet family, she chooses them as the subject of her ridicule. What impression do you think she is giving Mr Darcy of herself, however?

66/75	Miss Bingley
72/80	Mr Darcy

75 'Oh! yes. – Do . . .'
Throughout the book Jane Austen often links portrait to character. Here Miss Bingley is spitefully implying that the social inferiority of Elizabeth's relatives would be revealed if their portraits were hung next to Darcy's relations. She sarcastically states that Elizabeth's beauty could not be captured by a painter. Darcy agrees that her character could not easily be caught, although her beauty could.

74/76	Miss Bingley
72/76	Elizabeth
73/83	Social aspects

76 But Elizabeth, who . . .
Notice the contrast in wit between the two women. Miss Bingley resorts to heavy, laboured sarcasm to impress Darcy. Elizabeth makes a light and witty remark to defuse an embarrassing situation.

75/77	Miss Bingley
75/78	Elizabeth
62/79	Aspects of language

Characters and ideas
previous/next comment

Chapter 11

77 Miss Bingley's attention . . .

Miss Bingley's attempts to attract Mr Darcy are becoming ridiculous. Firstly, she talks nonsense about reading. Secondly, she flaunts her figure by walking around the room: still to no avail. Finally, she has to ask Elizabeth, the very object of her jealousy, to accompany her, in order to get Mr Darcy to look.

78 'Not at all,' . . .

Elizabeth understands Darcy here and knows exactly how to stand up to him. Miss Bingley, desperate to please, does not follow Elizabeth's advice to remain silent. Jane Austen sums up this fawning quality ironically when she says, 'Miss Bingley . . . was incapable of disappointing Mr Darcy in any . . . thing'. Elizabeth shows her better understanding of Mr Darcy later on the page when she suggests teasing and laughing as good methods of getting their own back.

79 'Certainly,' replied Elizabeth . . .

Elizabeth is the mouthpiece of Jane Austen. Consider the characters that she satirizes (Mr Collins and Miss Bingley). Do you agree that she merely mocks their foolishness and 'inconsistencies', or is she making a wider, social comment?

80 'Perhaps that is . . .'

Notice how seriously Darcy takes himself. He consciously tries to avoid putting himself into a situation where he is open to ridicule or teasing by a 'strong understanding' such as Elizabeth's.

81 'I am perfectly . . .'

Elizabeth teases Darcy about the self-awareness of his character. She is witty too about his self-confessed defect. How true is it, though, that he cannot forgive other people's 'offences' against him? In answering this, you should consider his behaviour towards Elizabeth when she has rejected his proposal, and also his behaviour towards Wickham after the elopement.

82 'And yours,' he . . .

Darcy acknowledges that Elizabeth is prejudiced against him. To what extent is her prejudice 'wilful', however?

Chapter 13

83 'Oh! my dear,' . . .

The laws of inheritance demanded that, on the death of the owner, the estate should be passed to a male relation. Thus Longbourn will go to Mr Collins, a distant cousin, and the Bennet daughters will be without fortune. Notice the childish way Mrs Bennet blames Mr Collins himself for this state of affairs, and therefore declares him to be 'odious'.

84 'Why, indeed, . . .'

Jane Austen frequently includes letters in her novel. Apart from carrying information, they are often a good indication of the character of the writer.

Characters and ideas	
previous/next	*comment*
76/78	Miss Bingley
77/121	Miss Bingley
76/79	Elizabeth
78/80	Elizabeth
76/88	Aspects of language
74/81	Mr Darcy
79/81	Elizabeth
80/95	Mr Darcy
80/92	Elizabeth
81/100	Elizabeth
71/101	Prejudice
61/85	Mr and Mrs Bennet
75/94	Social aspects
0/85	Mr Collins
68/95	Structure

What impression is given of Mr Collins's character? The Bennet family are divided as to his qualities. On the next page we see that Mrs Bennet is favourably impressed, even optimistic that he will be advantageous to the girls; Jane, more realistic than her mother, at least thinks it is worthy that he wishes to try and help.

It is left to Mr Bennet and Elizabeth to see the true man. She is not taken in by his pomposity, or impressed by his 'extraordinary deference for Lady Catherine'. Mr Bennet is not deceived either, but true to character he cannot help but be flippant about the man, 'There is a mixture of servility and self-importance . . .'.

85 'Ah! sir, I . . .'
Note Mrs Bennet's bluntness and total lack of tact. Anyone more sensitive than Mr Collins would find it very offensive to talk about the entailment in that way.

83/89	Mr and Mrs Bennet
84/86	Mr Collins

86 'I am very sensible, . . .'
His desire as expressed in the letter to make 'every possible amends' towards the daughters seems to imply that he is prepared to marry one of them. He announces that he has come 'prepared to admire them'.

85/87	Mr Collins
73/92	Love and marriage

Chapter 14

87 During dinner, . . .
What do you think of Lady de Bourgh, as here portrayed by Mr Collins? Is she doing any more than her duty? In what way do you think she is interfering too much? Do you think Mr Collins is too humble towards her?

86/88	Mr Collins
0/107	Lady Catherine

88 'She is a most . . .'
Notice how his choice of words demonstrates the obsequiousness of his character. Just the phrase, 'my humble abode', says so much about his view of Lady de Bourgh and her daughter, and their relationship with him.

87/89	Mr Collins
79/89	Aspects of language

89 'You judge very . . .'
How do we know Mr Bennet is being sarcastic here? Look at his comment on Mr Collins, 'flattering with delicacy'. Why does Mr Bennet enjoy Mr Collins's performance so much? Why is it significant that he should give the 'occasional glance' to his daughter?

85/93	Mr and Mrs Bennet
88/91	Mr Collins
88/94	Aspects of language

90 'Do you know, . . .'
What does it say about Lydia's and Kitty's characters that, far from listening to the serious work that Mr Collins is reading, they chat about the local officers?

44/248	Kitty and Mary
64/139	Lydia

Chapter 15

91 Mr Collins was not . . .
By way of a summary of our knowledge of the character of Mr Collins, Jane

89/92	Mr Collins

Austen describes him as 'a mixture of pride and obsequiousness, self-importance and humility'. Look back to the previous chapter to find examples of these characteristics.

92 Having now a . . .
What part does pride play in Mr Collins's decision to marry one of the Bennet girls? Why does he think they will have him? What does this say about his attitude to marriage? Notice the ironical tones with which Jane Austen describes his decision and subsequent behaviour. 'He thought it an excellent one, . . .'. On the next page look how she underlines the rapidity and lack of emotion with which he switches attention from Jane to Elizabeth. 'Mr Collins had only . . . done while Mrs Bennet was stirring the fire'!

91/96	Mr Collins
86/93	Love and marriage

93 Mrs Bennet treasured . . .
Note her total lack of discrimination and intelligence. Her sole concern is to find a husband with a fortune. It is quite inconsequential to her that the said man be quite incompatible with her daughter. It would not take much power of perception on her part to know that Elizabeth and Mr Collins were hardly the ideal match!

89/125	Mr and Mrs Bennet
92/15	Love and marriage

94 But the attention . . .
Notice the first impressions of the man, his 'gentlemanlike appearance', and further down 'His appearance was greatly in his favour'. He possesses all the attributes to make him attractive: beauty, pleasant manner, rank in the army. The repetition of the word 'appearance' is Jane Austen's first signal that Wickham is not necessarily the man he seems.

0/95	Mr Wickham
83/96	Social aspects
89/96	Aspects of language

95 But the attention . . .
A note of mystery and suspense is struck here. Why are Wickham and Darcy so surprised to see each other? We are left in the dark, for the moment.

94/99	Mr Wickham
81/104	Mr Darcy
84/118	Structure

96 Mrs Philips was . . .
Both Mr Collins and Mrs Philips are being satirized by Jane Austen for their emphasis on 'breeding'. Although the author does not dismiss good manners, Mr Collins and Mrs Philips are made to look silly by attaching too much importance to them. His remarks to Mrs Bennet about the sister, on the next page, are absurd in their exaggeration, and show that Mr Collins judges people superficially.

92/97	Mr Collins
94/97	Social aspects
94/98	Aspects of language

Chapter 16

97 When this information . . .
Mr Collins has a great interest in material trappings and the cost of everything. His comparison with Rosings, Lady de Bourgh's home, would seem insulting to a more sensitive ear. Jane Austen is satirizing the materialism of the people of this class.

96/98	Mr Collins
96/108	Social aspects

98 In describing to . . .
Notice his constant use of 'humble abode' (this is the third time) to describe

97/99	Mr Collins

his home. What does it say about his character that he has to keep repeating himself thus? Notice how subtly Jane Austen mocks him by the use of repetition.

99 With such rivals . . .
The attractiveness of Wickham is increased by his ease of conversation which is highlighted by the pedestrian nature of Collins's discourse.

100 'Oh! no – it . . .'
Wickham cunningly evokes Elizabeth's sympathy by the use of the emotive word 'scandalous'. Although too well-bred to ask any more questions on the subject she is curious to know more. It does not strike her that Wickham is being indiscreet in relating this story to a comparative stranger.

101 'Good heavens!' cried . . .
It shows the extent of Elizabeth's prejudice against Darcy that she is willing to believe Wickham's defamation of his character. She has suspended her usual scepticism and believes everything that Wickham tells her.

102 'Some time or . . .'
Wickham has cunningly let Elizabeth believe that he has not brought the matter out in public because of honourable considerations. Why does Elizabeth find Wickham's story so reasonable? Notice how Wickham feeds on Elizabeth's dislike of Darcy to convince her still further of the truth of his story.

103 Elizabeth was again . . .
The question of appearance and reality is relevant here. How far is Elizabeth more ready to believe Wickham's story because his 'countenance may vouch' for him 'being amiable'? In the same way how far does Darcy's 'forbidding, disagreeable countenance' as described in chapter 3, make it easier for her to form prejudice against him? Look at the comments on 'Social aspects' to see the relevance of 'appearance'.

104 'How strange!' cried . . .
Wickham blackens Darcy's character totally by accusing him of dishonour in failing to keep a promise. Elizabeth cannot believe that a gentleman of Darcy's standing could do such a thing. Surely, his pride, if nothing else, would make him behave honestly. By establishing their total loathing for each other, Wickham can now suggest that other 'impulses' such as jealousy and hatred have dominated Darcy's not inconsiderable pride.

105 'Yes. It has . . .'
Look how Wickham views Darcy's actions. He admits that Darcy acts generously towards his tenants and the poor, and lovingly towards his sister (all things which Elizabeth finds out for herself when she visits Pemberley), but with total cynicism he attributes them completely to pride. 'It has connected him nearer with virtue', he says at the bottom of the previous page.

Characters and ideas	
previous/next **comment**	
96/99	Aspects of language
95/100	Mr Wickham
98/112	Mr Collins
98/100	Aspects of language
99/101	Mr Wickham
82/101	Elizabeth
99/116	Aspects of language
100/102	Mr Wickham
82/102	Elizabeth
82/102	Prejudice
101/104	Mr Wickham
101/103	Elizabeth
101/103	Prejudice
102/110	Elizabeth
102/117	Prejudice
102/105	Mr Wickham
95/105	Mr Darcy
104/106	Mr Wickham
104/106	Mr Darcy
72/127	Pride

106 'Probably not;−. . .'
What total defamation of character! Adding to the list of damnable faults that Wickham says Darcy possesses he now adds hypocrisy! Answering Elizabeth's query about how an agreeable man such as Bingley can like such a bad character, Wickham maintains he behaves differently among his equals than he does with everyone else!

107 'Mr Collins,' said . . .
Notice how Elizabeth has already decided that Lady de Bourgh is an 'arrogant, conceited woman'. This is on the basis of Mr Collins's reports of her. Wickham describes her as deriving 'part of her abilities from her rank and fortune . . .'. Bear these assessments in mind when we meet her at Rosings.

108 Elizabeth allowed that . . .
Notice how Wickham gains the approval of everyone, particularly Elizabeth, because his manners are correct.

Chapter 17

109 'They have both,' . . .
True to character, look at how Jane reacts to Elizabeth's account of Wickham's story. She has to think well of Darcy to explain Bingham's regard for him. Rather than condemning Darcy she suggests that maybe the full story has not yet been told. For once, her attempt to see good in everyone is justified, for we have indeed only heard one version of the story.

110 'I can much more . . .'
Look how well Wickham has carried out his deception. How ironic are Elizabeth's words, 'there was truth in his looks'! She has been completely taken in by Wickham's appearance of virtue.

111 The prospect of . . .
Balls and dancing were the major social activity of this class especially when in the country. Notice the rules surrounding the ball; the sending of 'ceremonious' cards, the honour of a personal invitation. The ball would provide the main topic of conversation for a week beforehand and for days after.

112 Elizabeth's spirits . . .
Because of its social function, i.e. allowing young people to talk privately in public and the frivolity of the activity itself, dancing might in serious and very religious circles be thought of as immoral. Mr Collins, however, dismisses such ideas. Does he strike you as a very pious clergyman? Check that you really understand the meaning of pious!

Chapter 18

113 'I do not . . .'
In order to avoid Darcy, Wickham has not appeared in company. Look back to the conversation between Wickham and Elizabeth in chapter 16, to see how ironical this is.

114 But Elizabeth was . . .
The dance, although one of the chief ways a couple could talk fairly intimately in private, could also be the source of much misery if it involved a boring, tiresome partner. This, in effect, is Elizabeth's experience with Mr Collins. A contrast to this is her dance with Mr Darcy. Although she would never admit to enjoying it, look at the animation of the conversation.

115 When the dancing . . .
We get an idea of Charlotte's attitude towards marriage from her remarks to Elizabeth about Darcy. To her Darcy should not be dismissed in favour of Wickham because the former is 'a man of ten times his consequence'. In other words to her it is highly significant that Darcy is by far the richer of the two.

116 'It is *your* turn . . .'
Elizabeth's comment on the self-consciousness of language is perceptive as far as she is concerned. She is very aware of the effectiveness of language as a tool of wit. Look back to chapter 9 – 'And so ended . . .' and chapter 10 – 'This walk is not . . .', for examples of this. Whether this is true also of Darcy is debatable.

117 Darcy made no . . .
A point in Darcy's favour, that Elizabeth fails to grasp, is his reluctance, or even refusal, to put his side of the story. Still blinded by prejudice, she does not see this as anything virtuous.

118 'I have been . . .'
Sir William Lucas is as unctuous as ever towards Darcy. Why is Darcy so alarmed by his assumption that Jane and Bingham are to be married? What effect does this news have on the continuation of the plot?

119 'And never allow . . .'
Elizabeth's statement is unconsciously ironic. It is she that should take heed of her own words, 'It is particularly incumbent . . .'.

120 'I can readily . . .'
Jane Austen uses the image of a picture to describe character. Notice her use of the words, 'illustration', 'sketch', 'likeness' in Elizabeth's attempts to assess Darcy's character.

121 'Insolent girl!' . . .
Why does Elizabeth not believe Miss Bingley? What motives does she suspect Miss Bingley to have in telling this to her?

Characters and ideas
previous/next comment

110/117	Mr Wickham
110/116	Elizabeth
111/123	Social aspects
32/137	Charlotte
93/125	Love and marriage
114/119	Elizabeth
100/120	Aspects of language
113/122	Mr Wickham
106/118	Mr Darcy
103/122	Prejudice
117/151	Mr Darcy
95/131	Structure
116/121	Elizabeth
116/128	Aspects of language
78/132	Miss Bingley
119/122	Elizabeth

122 'I have not a . . .'
So complete is her prejudice against Darcy and in favour of Wickham that Elizabeth will not even trust Bingley's mildly critical report against Wickham's character.

117/200	Mr Wickham
121/127	Elizabeth
117/148	Prejudice

123 'Indeed I am . . .'
Mr Collins, with his strange mixture of 'self-importance and humility', is anxious to meet Darcy because of their mutual connection. Elizabeth, fearing that Darcy will regard it as 'impertinent freedom', underlines Darcy's pride. Also she knows that the strict etiquette of the time demands formal introduction. Mr Collins believes that his status as a clergyman places him 'as equal in point of dignity'.

112/124	Mr Collins
114/149	Social aspects

124 'My dear Miss . . .'
What does it say about Mr Collins's sensitivity that he does not appreciate the scorn with which Mr Darcy treats him?

123/128	Mr Collins

125 As Elizabeth had . . .
Notice Mrs Bennet's terrible indiscretion in discussing the possibility of marriage between her daughter and Bingley. Unknown to her, she is the cause of the disruption in the relationship as Darcy, alarmed by the schemes and plans he overhears, persuades his friend to leave quickly for London.

93/126	Mr and Mrs Bennet
115/128	Love and marriage

126 'If I,' said Mr . . .
The contrast in sensitivity between the two is marked by their differing reactions to Mr Collins's boring and inappropriate speech. Mr Bennet, whose liking for the absurd and incongruous is immense, enjoys it thoroughly. Mrs Bennet, who takes everything and everyone at face value, approves whole-heartedly.

125/130	Mr and Mrs Bennet

127 To Elizabeth it . . .
Although it is because of her higher degree of sensitivity that she is aware of the social awkwardness of her family, what does it say about her pride that it matters how her family behaves? Why does she care about the opinion of Darcy and Bingley's two sisters?

122/129	Elizabeth
105/179	Pride

Chapter 19

128 'My reasons for . . .'
After the long list of sensible reasons why he should marry, why is his statement, '. . . nothing remains for me but to assure you . . .' so incongruous and so funny?

124/155	Mr Collins
125/130	Love and marriage
120/158	Aspects of language

129 'Upon my word, . . .'
Notice the dramatic irony in Elizabeth's words, 'Nay, were your friend Lady Catherine . . .'. How do the two get on, especially when Lady Catherine visits Longbourn?

107/160	Lady Catherine
127/133	Elizabeth

Chapter 20

130 'Aye, there she . . .'
Behind Mrs Bennet's comical attempts to force Elizabeth to marry there are real fears based on economics. How would Elizabeth manage on the death of Mr Bennet, if she had not secured a successful partner?

| 126/140 | Mr and Mrs Bennet |
| 18/136 | Love and marriage |

Chapter 21

131 'This is from . . .'
This letter had a dual function. It reveals still further Caroline Bingley's unkind and malicious character. It creates suspense and tension in the plot as it drives Jane and Bingley apart.

| 118/153 | Structure |

132 'Why will you . . .'
What kind of woman is Miss Bingley who can write ideas of this kind in a letter knowing that they will deeply hurt the recipient?

| 121/241 | Miss Bingley |

133 'What think you . . .'
Look at the way the two sisters differ in their response to the letter. Jane believes everything Caroline says. Elizabeth, who is more perceptive, suspects that malice and self-interest have driven Miss Bingley to write what is no more than hopeful thinking on her part.

| 109/134 | Jane |
| 129/138 | Elizabeth |

134 'If we thought . . .'
Jane's good nature refuses to allow her to accept that Miss Bingley's motives could be anything but worthy.

| 133/140 | Jane |

135 'But if he returns . . .'
Interestingly neither Jane nor Elizabeth fully realize the extent of Bingley's compliant character. Jane maintains 'he is his own master' – chapter 21, and even astute Elizabeth is confident that it would be difficult to 'influence a young man so totally independent of everyone'.

| 70/238 | Mr Bingley |

Chapter 22

136 In as short . . .
The reasons why Charlotte Lucas accepts Mr Collins's proposal are made quite plain: they are purely economic. Hence her parents' joy at such a good match. Notice how Jane Austen mocks their calculating ways of working out when the daughter will be mistress of Longbourn!

| 37/162 | The Lucases |
| 130/137 | Love and marriage |

137 Sir William and . . .
Charlotte goes into this marriage with her eyes wide open. She knows Mr Collins's faults, indeed finds his company 'irksome', but she is gaining something she prizes above happiness. She is gaining security and comfort. Marriage 'was the only honourable provision . . .'. Rather than finding the situation intolerable she regards herself as lucky. Look at the end of chapter 22, and how she sums up her situation to Elizabeth.

| 115/158 | Charlotte |
| 136/138 | Love and marriage |

Characters and ideas previous/next comment

138 Elizabeth quietly answered . . .
Elizabeth is shocked at what she regards as Charlotte's mercenary motives for marrying; this, plus a conviction that Charlotte could not possibly be happy with a man like Mr Collins, makes her unhappy.

Chapter 23

139 Elizabeth was sitting . . .
Who does Lydia remind you of with her 'uncivil' and 'unguarded' remark?

140 Mrs Bennet was in . . .
Notice how true to character each of the Bennet family is in their reaction to the news: Mrs Bennet rants and raves; Mr Bennet is cynical; Jane wishes them well; Kitty and Lydia are uninterested in it except for its gossip value.

141 Even Elizabeth began . . .
Mrs Bennet's obsession with getting her daughters married really does bring out the worst in her character. Look at the insensitive way she treats Jane's feelings, and at the suspicion she attributes to Charlotte's and Mrs Lucas's behaviour. She really shows how small-minded she is.

Chapter 24

142 Elizabeth, to whom . . .
One of Elizabeth's most endearing qualities is her loyalty and regard towards Jane. Her more astute nature leads her to play a protective role towards her naïve, trusting sister. See here how concerned she is about the effect Bingley's scheming sisters will have on her own dear sister's happiness.

143 'Oh! that my dear . . .'
How would you summarize Jane's interpretation of Bingley's absence? Are Jane's assumptions about Bingley's feelings typical of her own unassuming character?

144 'Nay,' said Elizabeth . . .
Elizabeth's disappointment in Bingley's behaviour and her friend Charlotte's too, arises from the realization that you cannot judge people by appearance. Ironically she has not yet realized that this might also apply to her opinion of Darcy and Wickham.

145 'To oblige you, . . .'
Look at Elizabeth's idealistic view of marriage. She finds it abhorrent that Charlotte can marry a man she cannot possibly like. Jane tries, in her usual understanding way, to explain the practical issues that persuaded Charlotte to make this decision. Elizabeth views this idea of marriage to be unprincipled, dangerous and selfish and lacking in integrity.

146 'I am far from . . .'
In the discussion of Bingley's motives for his absence we see the character of
the two girls highlighted. Who is the more astute here? How does Jane's
belief in the goodness of people cloud her judgement here? Why would she
prefer to believe that she was mistaken about Bingley's feelings, rather than
accept that he is being guided by his sisters to a superior match?

143/148   Jane
145/151   Elizabeth

147 Mr Bennet treated . . .
Notice Mr Bennet's flippant attitude to Jane's position. What does this tell
you about the depth of his feeling for his family?

141/155   Mr and Mrs
          Bennet

148 Mr Wickham's society . . .
The popularity of Wickham reinforces the general bad opinion of Darcy.
Only Jane refuses to judge him on the basis of prejudice and rumour.

146/156   Jane
122/152   Prejudice

Chapter 25

149 On the following . . .
The Gardiners represent the sensible side of Mrs Bennet's family. The part
they play in bringing together Elizabeth and Darcy is significant. Look at
chapter 43 – 'The introduction, however, . . .', to see how Darcy's opinion of
Elizabeth's background changes on their acquaintance.

0/253   The Gardiners
123/151   Social
          aspects

150 When alone with . . .
In Mrs Gardiner's comment is revealed Jane Austen's condemnation of
romantic love as being too fragile a basis for marriage.

145/154   Love and
          marriage

151 'And *that* is quite . . . '
Note Elizabeth's heavy sarcasm as she mocks one of Darcy's greatest faults,
his snobbery.

118/172   Mr Darcy
146/154   Elizabeth
149/163   Social
          aspects

152 Mrs Gardiner had . . .
Look what a subtly persuasive quality is prejudice. Although she cannot
remember Darcy's character well she allows herself to be convinced that she
recalled him to be 'a very proud ill-natured boy'.

148/176   Prejudice

153 Mrs Gardiner had . . .
Notice how this chapter and the previous one end on the same note of
disapproval of Darcy. What is Jane Austen making absolutely clear in our
minds before the dramatic climax of the proposal?

131/156   Structure

Chapter 26

154 'You are too . . .'
Notice again the importance of fortune in a marriage. What do you think of

151/160   Elizabeth

Elizabeth's answer to her aunt's advice on the next page? Look at the end of the chapter to see how philosophically Elizabeth accepts Wickham's desertion.

150/158	Love and marriage

155 Mr Collins returned . . .
Notice Mrs Bennet's lack of civility in regard to Mr Collins. Why is she so ungracious?

147/217	Mr and Mrs Bennet
128/158	Mr Collins

156 My dearest Lizzy, . . .
Note the use of the letter to show a development in character. Jane comes to learn painfully of the deceitful character of Miss Bingley.

148/189	Jane
153/157	Structure

Chapter 27

157 Before they were . . .
Notice how cleverly Jane Austen matches Elizabeth's low mood with an awkward moment for the smooth development of the plot. The relationship between Jane and Bingley seems to be over; the suspense as to whom Mr Collins will marry has gone; Wickham has lost interest in Elizabeth; general opinion of Darcy's low character is established. A change of scene is needed to cheer up Elizabeth and to set the plot into motion once again.

156/173	Structure

Chapter 28

158 At length the Parsonage . . .
Note again how Jane Austen satirizes Mr Collins with the repetition of 'humble abode'. Note too Elizabeth's sceptical assessment of the Collins's household. She senses that Mr Collins is trying to show her what grand things she lost by refusing his proposal and she feels that Charlotte, although cheerful, makes her own happiness by assuring as much distance as she can between herself and Mr Collins as often as possible. Look two paragraphs on in the text at the comment Elizabeth makes for confirmation of this idea.

155/159	Mr Collins
137/0	Charlotte
154/188	Love and marriage
128/162	Aspects of language

159 Elizabeth was prepared . . .
How does Mr Collins assess the value of surroundings and nature? Look how everything is quantified and numbered rather than appreciated for its own sake. Jane Austen mocks him for his lack of sensitivity to beauty, 'every view was pointed out with a minuteness which left beauty entirely behind'. Look at chapter 29 – 'From the entrance . . .', to see how he does the same to Rosings.

158/162	Mr Collins

160 'And is this . . .'
Note the sarcasm of Elizabeth's comment. What does it reveal about her attitude to Lady de Bourgh and her daughter? Do you think she would agree with Mr Collins's comment on the previous page that Lady de Bourgh 'is the sort of woman whom one cannot regard with too much deference'?

129/163	Lady Catherine
154/161	Elizabeth

161 'I like her appearance . . .'
Elizabeth is pleased at Miss de Bourgh's 'sickly and cross' appearance. Who is she referring to when she sarcastically says 'She will make him a very proper wife'?

160/164   Elizabeth

Chapter 29

162 Mr Collins's triumph . . .
Notice the mixture of humility and pomposity that both Mr Collins and Sir William share. Notice also how Jane Austen mocks Sir William and the self-consciousness of his new status.

136/164   The Lucases
159/163   Mr Collins
158/168   Aspects of language

163 'Do not make . . .'
What does the sentence 'She likes to have the distinction of rank preserved' tell you about Lady de Bourgh's character, and about Mr Collins's too?

162/171   Mr Collins
160/165   Lady Catherine
151/164   Social aspects

164 When they ascended . . .
Contrast the feelings of the Lucases with those of Elizabeth as they prepare to meet Lady de Bourgh. Why is Elizabeth not in awe? What does it say about the amount of importance she attaches to rank?

162/0   The Lucases
161/165   Elizabeth
163/169   Social aspects

165 In spite of having . . .
Look at the contrast in the way the Lucases and Elizabeth behave before Lady de Bourgh. What later episode, in particular, demonstrates that Elizabeth is indeed 'quite equal to the scene' of being presented to Lady Catherine?

163/166   Lady Catherine
164/176   Elizabeth

166 In spite of having . . .
Look back to the end of chapter 16, to see how Elizabeth's impressions of Lady de Bourgh match Wickham's.

165/167   Lady Catherine

167 The dinner was . . .
What do you think of a person who enjoys constant and 'excessive admiration'?

166/168   Lady Catherine

168 When the ladies . . .
Notice how Jane Austen uses dialogue to develop a point she has made about character. She says that 'Elizabeth felt all the impertinence of her (Lady de Bourgh's) questions'. How does Elizabeth show on the next page that she does regard the questions as 'impertinent'? Note the brevity of her answers.

167/170   Lady Catherine
162/170   Aspects of language

169 'No governess! . . .'
Notice the informal attitude to education that was prevalent at that time, particularly where girls were concerned. Which two of the Bennet daughters do you think 'chose to be idle'?

Chapter 30

170 Elizabeth soon perceived . . .
Why is Jane's description of Lady de Bourgh as 'this great lady' ironic? How does her behaviour towards the Collinses and other village people reveal that she is quite the opposite?

Chapter 31

171 The invitation was . . .
What is Lady de Bourgh's impression of Mr Collins? Do you think he is aware of this?

172 Colonel Fitzwilliam seemed . . .
What effect would this ease of conversation between Elizabeth and Colonel Fitzwilliam have on Mr Darcy?

173 Colonel Fitzwilliam seemed . . .
Elizabeth finds Fitzwilliam an interesting, knowledgeable person to talk to. In every way he is unlike his cousin, easy in company, with a pleasant, conversational manner. His role in the plot is to increase Darcy's interest in Elizabeth in the form of jealousy.

174 'So much the better . . .'
Once again dialogue is used to confirm character that has previously been described. Here Lady de Bourgh shows herself at her most interfering thus revealing her lack of breeding, and snobbery.

175 Mr Darcy looked . . .
Notice again the clever use of contrast. Darcy was offended by lack of breeding on Elizabeth's side of the family. Now his relative is showing her lack of manners. The reader can sense a softening in his attitude to Elizabeth and an increased interest on her part towards him.

Characters and ideas
previous/next comment

164/170	Social aspects
168/171	Lady Catherine
169/174	Social aspects
168/174	Aspects of language
163/209	Mr Collins
170/174	Lady Catherine
151/175	Mr Darcy
0/183	Fitzwilliam
157/175	Structure
171/206	Lady Catherine
170/175	Social aspects
170/191	Aspects of language
172/176	Mr Darcy
173/182	Structure
174/178	Social aspects

	Characters and ideas previous/next comment

176 'You mean to frighten . . .'
The wit and repartee in the dialogue between Elizabeth and Darcy reveals the attraction there is between them, even though her prejudice will not allow her to see it herself.

175/178	Mr Darcy
165/177	Elizabeth
152/177	Prejudice

177 Elizabeth laughed heartily . . .
Elizabeth raises the question of appearance and reality here. Jokingly she regrets that Darcy's presence will prevent her from putting forward a false front in public. He will be able to expose her 'real character'. To what extent does Darcy know her 'real' character? Has her prejudice against him not already led her to present a false picture of herself? You should be able to give textual references to support your views.

176/180	Elizabeth
176/181	Prejudice

178 'You shall hear . . .'
Elizabeth, in a teasing way, criticizes Darcy for disobeying the strict etiquette of the day, which expects that a gentleman will show the agreeability of his character by dancing, especially if there are many available young ladies.

176/179	Mr Darcy
175/180	Social aspects

179 'My fingers,' said . . .
Neither Elizabeth nor Fitzwilliam will accept that shyness is a good enough excuse for Darcy's haughtiness. Teasingly, Elizabeth suggests that it is not fitting for a man in his position to hide behind such an excuse. Practice will improve his condition.

178/180	Mr Darcy
127/192	Pride

180 Darcy smiled and . . .
'We neither of us perform to strangers', the notion of performance as a necessary part of social life is a theme running throughout the book. You must appear to behave in an expected way in order to be socially acceptable. Darcy has the scorn of public opinion brought down on him because he fails to do this. On what occasions does Elizabeth fail to 'perform' in the correct manner? Look at chapter 10 – the invitation to dance a reel, for her unexpected remarks to Mr Darcy and the interview in chapter 56 with Lady de Bourgh.

179/181	Mr Darcy
177/181	Elizabeth
178/188	Social aspects

Chapter 32

181 Mr Darcy drew . . .
Note the way Darcy draws his chair nearer, a sign of his desire to get to know Elizabeth better. Note also his remark, 'You cannot have been . . .'. Look back to chapter 9, to find out his opinion of country people. The liveliness of Elizabeth's mind has made a great impression on him and helped to clear away some of his prejudices.

180/182	Mr Darcy
180/184	Elizabeth
177/184	Prejudice

182 But why Mr Darcy . . .
Notice how Jane Austen uses Charlotte to voice the reader's own queries as to Darcy's motives here. The tension is being built up towards the climax of the proposal.

181/192	Mr Darcy
175/183	Structure

183 In her kind . . .
Colonel Fitzwilliam's presence acts to increase the tension. His outgoing, agreeable personality is a contrast to Darcy's more cold and controlled manner, and leads the reader to conjecture if he is not a more suitable choice for Elizabeth.

173/186 Fitzwilliam
182/184 Structure

Chapter 33

184 More than once . . .
Notice how Jane Austen keeps up the tension and suspense, by making it quite clear to the reader that Darcy has fallen in love with Elizabeth. Yet Elizabeth is still so blind, so incorrect in her interpretation of Darcy's motives!

181/187 Elizabeth
181/187 Prejudice
183/185 Structure

185 As she spoke . . .
Notice the closely woven details of the plot. Here Jane Austen is making reference to an event that we, the readers, are yet ignorant of, i.e. Wickham's attempted seduction of Darcy's sister.

184/186 Structure

186 'And remember that . . .'
Fitzwilliam's function here is to provide Elizabeth with information about Bingley that she could not otherwise obtain. The knowledge that Darcy has indeed been the source of Jane's unhappiness by persuading Bingley to leave Netherfield is guaranteed to upset Elizabeth and set her completely against Darcy. The tension then is at its height for the proposal.

183/0 Fitzwilliam
185/190 Structure

187 This was spoken . . .
Elizabeth's prejudices are confirmed, she blames Darcy's pride and she is deeply wounded. Her reading of Jane's letter on the next page ensures a very high state of indignation towards Darcy. In total it does not bode well for Darcy's proposal.

184/189 Elizabeth
184/198 Prejudice

188 'There were some . . .'
Notice the importance of 'connections' in determining a marriage. Elizabeth is convinced that it is this factor and not their mother's lack of breeding that chiefly convinced Darcy to persuade Bingley against a marriage with Jane.

158/210 Love and
         marriage
180/194 Social
         aspects

Chapter 34

189 When they were . . .
Elizabeth is able to make use of Jane's letters to kindle the fire of her indignation towards Darcy.

156/213 Jane
187/193 Elizabeth

190 'In vain have I . . .'
We have seen how Jane Austen has built up the atmosphere of hostility towards Darcy before his proposal. Hence the declaration of love comes as a complete shock to Elizabeth, who, blinded by her prejudice, has been ignorant of his increased interest.

191 Elizabeth's astonishment . . .
Notice that Jane Austen chooses not to use conversation to narrate Darcy's proposal. The use of narrative here allows her to make known Elizabeth's feelings towards his proposal simultaneously with his speaking. Notice the contrast in style as Elizabeth replies.

192 In spite of her . . .
Has Darcy's character changed? What two aspects of his proposal convince Elizabeth that his pride has not altered? Read the text carefully!

193 'In such cases as . . .'
What aspect of the proposal has hurt Elizabeth more than anything?

194 As she pronounced . . .
Why should Elizabeth's words have had such an impact on him? Why would the charge of ungentlemanly behaviour be a serious matter for Darcy? In answering this question be aware of the comments made about the social aspects to the background of this novel.

195 'I have every . . .'
Note the importance of social opinion here. Elizabeth blames Darcy, not merely because he has broken up a possible love match, but also because he has made two people lose esteem in the face of society.

196 'And this,' cried . . .
Do you think Darcy is justified in thinking that Elizabeth's family was a just impediment to him making up his mind about marrying her? Don't forget the social context of the novel.

Chapter 35

197 Be not alarmed . . .
What is the function of the letter in regard to the plot? Note how some new information in it sets off a change in Elizabeth. How does the letter indicate that Darcy himself has begun to change?

Chapter 36

198 If Elizabeth, . . .
Notice that the first reading of the letter leaves Elizabeth unchanged in her prejudice and hostility against Darcy. She still cannot admit that he is correct

Characters and ideas *previous*/*next* comment	
186/197	Structure
174/209	Aspects of language
182/194	Mr Darcy
179/204	Pride
189/197	Elizabeth
192/196	Mr Darcy
188/195	Social aspects
194/196	Social aspects
194/197	Mr Darcy
195/201	Social aspects
196/200	Mr Darcy
193/198	Elizabeth
190/212	Structure
197/199	Elizabeth
187/199	Prejudice

about Jane or her family. It is only when the matter concerning Wickham is understood that she admits the justice of his views about Jane and her family.

199 But when this subject . . .
It is the story of Wickham which begins to crack the shell of Elizabeth's prejudice against Darcy. She realizes that both versions cannot be true. Whose is she to believe? Note the powerful emotions with which this realization hits her, 'Astonishment, apprehension and even horror'.

198/201	Elizabeth	
198/202	Prejudice	

200 In this perturbed . . .
Look back to chapter 16, for Wickham's account of the will. Now look at chapter 35, to find Darcy's account. How do the two differ?

122/201	Mr Wickham	
197/203	Mr Darcy	

201 The extravagance and . . .
In her struggle to decide which of the two men is telling the truth, note again the importance which public opinion has in forming her attitude to Wickham in the first place.

200/202	Mr Wickham	
199/202	Elizabeth	
196/208	Social aspects	

202 She perfectly remembered . . .
Notice, now that the veil of prejudice has fallen as far as Wickham is concerned, how she gradually reinterprets his behaviour and comes up with an entirely different view of his character. Firstly she acknowledges his lack of good taste in talking to her, a stranger, about his private life; next she realizes his absence from the ball is due to cowardice; finally she recalls the way he slandered Darcy's character in his absence. Look at the next page to see how different his character appears in this light.

201/221	Mr Wickham	
201/203	Elizabeth	
199/203	Prejudice	

203 How differently . . .
Just as the letter has forced her to reappraise Wickham so does she now look anew at the character of Darcy. She has to admit that nothing in his behaviour ever showed him to be 'unprincipled or unjust'. With great emotion does she realize that she has been 'blind, partial, prejudiced, absurd'.

200/215	Mr Darcy	
202/204	Elizabeth	
202/218	Prejudice	

204 She grew absolutely . . .
This is the turning point for Elizabeth in her search for self-realization. She blames her lack of perception on her pride which was flattered by the attention of Wickham and offended by the impoliteness of Darcy.

203/205	Elizabeth	
192/205	Pride	

205 From herself to Jane – . . .
When pride has been swept away she has to admit that Darcy's comments on Jane's seeming lack of affection for Bingley, and her family's tactless behaviour at the ball, are true.

204/207	Elizabeth	
204/207	Pride	

Chapter 37

206 Their first subject . . .
Only the reader (and Elizabeth) understand the irony of her statement. She supposes it is herself or her daughter that Darcy is reluctant to leave. The sense of her own importance and her dictatorial nature are apparent on the next page as she tries to persuade Elizabeth to stay.

207 Mr Darcy's letter . . .
Although Elizabeth shows respect and gratitude to Darcy she has not yet come to like him, as she is still offended by his proud and haughty manner. It is not until they meet again at Pemberley that she overcomes this obstacle.

208 Anxiety on Jane's . . .
Bitterly, Elizabeth accepts the shortcomings of her family. Look back to the previous page in the text to see a list of their failings. It is her family's lack of breeding that she accepts is the main cause of Jane's sad situation.

Chapter 38

209 'It gives me . . .'
His pomposity is apparent in his way of speaking, but his lack of insight is well summed up in the last sentence where the reader understands the irony of his words 'our intimacy at Rosings'. He is so insensitive that he has not understood that their company is only required when there is no one better around. His insensitivity is also evident on the next page when referring to himself and Charlotte he says, 'We seem to have been designed for each other'.

210 Elizabeth could safely . . .
Although Elizabeth can see Charlotte is relatively content she still does not approve of the marriage. Her phrase 'had not yet lost their charms' is very telling. Her assumption is that eventually the novelty of her new life and its surroundings will wear off and Charlotte will come face to face with the man she has married.

Chapter 39

211 'And we mean . . .'
What does it say about Lydia's character that her main preoccupation is spending money on inessentials and concerning herself solely with the issue of whether soldiers or other gentlemen will be in the locality?

212 'How nicely we . . .'
This chapter is a prelude to the next event in the story, Lydia's elopement. See how we are prepared for such an event by knowing of her desire to marry, her liking for Wickham and especially her complete lack of any common sense or depth of thought. She is incapable of thinking seriously about anything.

Characters and ideas previous/next comment

174/285	Lady Catherine
205/208	Elizabeth
205/221	Pride
207/210	Elizabeth
201/214	Social aspects
171/254	Mr Collins
191/222	Aspects of language
208/215	Elizabeth
188/224	Love and marriage
140/212	Lydia
211/220	Lydia
197/216	Structure

Chapter 40

213 She then spoke . . .
Her reaction to the truth about the Wickham affair is typical. Incapable of believing ill of anybody, she endeavours to find a way that will show both Darcy and Wickham to be honourable men.

214 'There certainly was . . .'
'One has got all the goodness, and the other . . .', the theme of appearance and reality is a major one in the book. The ease with which even discerning people like Elizabeth can be deceived was a danger prevalent in Jane Austen's society, where people were judged on their manners and breeding, and where a strict code of public behaviour was expected. This behaviour could be easily imitated as it was their 'performance' on which they were judged.

215 'And yet I meant . . .'
Disliking Darcy was a 'spur' to Elizabeth's 'genius' she says. Look back at past conversations between Darcy and Elizabeth (chapters 6 and 10). How far do you think she actually enjoyed disliking him?

216 'That it ought . . .'
Elizabeth's decision to say nothing publicly about her changed opinion of Wickham and Darcy has dire consequences for the family, and therefore it was important for the plot that she did keep silent. Had her parents known of Wickham's true character would they have been so lenient towards Lydia?

217 'Oh well! it is . . .'
Mrs Bennet reveals her lack of understanding in two ways here. She is not sympathetic to Jane's predicament but instead makes childish statements about making Bingley pay. She is equally foolish in her attitude to Mr Collins, blaming him for the conditions of entailment.

Chapter 41

218 Such were the . . .
Notice that now that the veil of prejudice has been dropped Elizabeth is beginning to see her family through Darcy's eyes. Their shallowness, until now a source of amusement to her, is beginning to embarrass her. She can even see why Darcy persuaded Bingley against them!

219 'Lydia will never . . .'
Look at the tone of Mr Bennet's reply. He answers sarcastically and unhelpfully to Elizabeth's plea that the reputation of the whole family is at stake. Only when Elizabeth really implores him to look seriously at the situation does he answer more sensibly (see the next page). This scene reveals the increasing maturity of Elizabeth and it stands out in contrast to the irresponsibility of her father.

Characters and ideas previous/next comment

previous/next	comment
189/249	Jane
208/223	Social aspects
203/223	Mr Darcy
210/218	Elizabeth
212/224	Structure
155/219	Mr and Mrs Bennet
215/219	Elizabeth
203/226	Prejudice
217/225	Mr and Mrs Bennet
218/221	Elizabeth

220 Had Lydia and . . .
This passage summarizes Lydia's character. It emphasizes her vanity, flirtatiousness and interest in only superficial matters.

221 Elizabeth was now . . .
As another step towards her attachment to Darcy, Elizabeth has to untie the threads that linked her to Wickham. Looking at him in a different light, the qualities that first made him attractive change. Her pride too is touched now that she knows his attention towards her is 'idle and frivolous'.

222 While she spoke, . . .
Notice Elizabeth's skill with words which alerts Wickham to the possibility that she might well know the true story. She implies this without actually saying as much. He is forced to listen to her 'with an apprehensive and anxious attention'.

223 'You, who so well . . .'
Wickham tries to explain the improvement in Darcy's behaviour by suggesting that he had adopted 'the appearance' of correct behaviour. The irony is that it is he, not Darcy, who has done just this.

Chapter 42

224 Had Elizabeth's opinion . . .
For Mr Bennet, the experience of marriage has been an unhappy one. Jane Austen, warning against marriages based on 'youth and beauty' and a semblance of 'good humour', suggests that such marriages are likely to falter. What is the significance of placing this observation at this point in the book? In answering the question, consider the various marriages and relationships described so far, and those to come.

225 Had Elizabeth's opinion . . .
To what extent does the account of Mr Bennet's marriage explain his cynical and sarcastic attitude to his family? Elizabeth feels that his contemptuous attitude towards his wife is a harmful example to his children. She does not think an unhappy marriage excuses him from being a dutiful father.

Chapter 43

226 'And of this . . .'
Elizabeth cannot help but think that this beautiful house could have been hers. How does her comment on the way she feels the Gardiners would be received by him reveal that her prejudice against Darcy has not yet altered? Look at chapter 43, to see how Darcy does treat them. Why is Elizabeth surprised?

Characters and ideas previous/next comment	
212/246	Lydia
202/222	Mr Wickham
219/222	Elizabeth
207/228	Pride
221/223	Mr Wickham
221/225	Elizabeth
209/252	Aspects of language
222/245	Mr Wickham
215/226	Mr Darcy
214/235	Social aspects
210/225	Love and marriage
216/231	Structure
219/247	Mr and Mrs Bennet
222/226	Elizabeth
224/239	Love and marriage
223/228	Mr Darcy
225/227	Elizabeth
218/227	Prejudice

	Characters and ideas previous/*next* comment

227 'Yes, Sir, I know . . .'
Another vital step in changing Elizabeth's prejudiced view of Darcy is the housekeeper's account of his character and behaviour. Elizabeth is astonished for her own view of Darcy is so unlike that of the housekeeper's.

226/230   Elizabeth
226/232   Prejudice

228 'He is the best . . .'
The housekeeper interprets Darcy's 'pride' as reserve, a refusal to 'rattle away like other young men'. Look back to chapter 3, to see if this is strictly true.

226/229   Mr Darcy
221/232   Pride

229 On reaching the . . .
The one quality that has never been in doubt about his nature is his care of his sister.

228/230   Mr Darcy

230 In the gallery . . .
What is the significance of the picture? How does it reinforce this new image of Darcy that has been presented to her at Pemberley? Notice on the next page how the contemplation of this portrait evokes new feelings towards Darcy.

229/234   Mr Darcy
227/231   Elizabeth

231 They were within . . .
Note the perfect timing of the plot. Here we see Elizabeth, who is mellowed by her reconsideration of Darcy, suddenly brought face to face with him. What factors cause her confusion?

230/233   Elizabeth
224/238   Structure

232 She had instinctively . . .
How far is the change in Darcy due to a modification of his own proud behaviour and how far is it due to a shift in Elizabeth's own feelings towards him? Is it his 'pride' or her 'prejudice' that has altered?

228/237   Pride
227/296   Prejudice

233 The others then . . .
Why is Elizabeth so concerned about being discovered at Pemberley? Of what motives does she think Darcy will suspect her?

231/234   Elizabeth

234 They had now . . .
What does it reveal about Elizabeth's present feelings towards Darcy that she is so concerned about whether or not he still cares for her?

230/236   Mr Darcy
233/235   Elizabeth

235 Mrs Gardiner was . . .
Note here again the importance of 'breeding' in that society. Why is Elizabeth so pleased that Darcy seems to get on so well with her aunt and uncle?

234/236   Elizabeth
223/236   Social aspects

236 The conversation soon . . .
Elizabeth is surprised at Darcy's new civil manner, is surprised that he still seems to care for her and is now astonished that he should wish her to meet his sister, an event of particular significance in those days.

234/237   Mr Darcy
235/237   Elizabeth
235/252   Social aspects

Chapter 44

237 Miss Darcy and . . .
Is not Miss Darcy's temperament essentially the same as her brother's? Look at the different interpretation that Elizabeth puts on her so-called 'pride'.

236/239	Mr Darcy
236/240	Elizabeth
232/297	Pride

238 Elizabeth was pleased . . .
Bingley hints that he still holds Jane in regard and regrets not having seen her for a long time. Elizabeth is heartened. This aspect of the plot, i.e. Jane and Bingley's relationship, left in the background for so long, begins to gather pace again.

135/277	Mr Bingley
231/291	Structure

239 It was not often . . .
Elizabeth cannot get over the change in Darcy's character. What do you think of her conclusion that such a change can only be caused by 'love, ardent love' (chapter 44)?

237/243	Mr Darcy
225/240	Love and marriage

240 Of Mr Darcy it . . .
The analysis of Elizabeth's feelings is typical of Jane Austen's rational approach to love. Elizabeth admits that she no longer hates Darcy, or even dislikes him. His good reputation and his civil manner make her respect him. The knowledge that he still loves her after her shameful rejection of his proposal, makes her grateful towards him. Respect and gratitude are the basis of a good marriage although Elizabeth is not yet ready to commit herself to that extent.

237/243	Elizabeth
239/244	Love and marriage

Chapter 45

241 'Pray, Miss Eliza . . .'
Although Miss Bingley does not know the connection between Wickham and Miss Darcy and is therefore ignorant of the embarrassment she causes, she intentionally sets out to unnerve Elizabeth. This chapter is a fine study of the jealousy in Miss Bingley's character which 'gave no one any pain but herself', (chapter 45).

132/242	Miss Bingley

242 Persuaded as Miss . . .
Look at the way she is content to defame her own character simply to gain the satisfaction (and the 'pain') of knowing that she has 'nettled' Darcy.

241/0	Miss Bingley

Chapter 46

243 Darcy made no . . .
How does Elizabeth interpret Darcy's silence? Judging him by his subsequent behaviour in regard to Wickham – look at chapter 52, what thoughts were more likely to be in his mind at this time?

239/244	Mr Darcy
240/244	Elizabeth

*Characters and ideas
previous/next comment*

244 Darcy made no . . .
The fear that the scandal surrounding Lydia's elopement will turn Darcy against Elizabeth crystallizes her feelings for him. Ironically she knows she could love him but now 'all love must be in vain'.

243/264	Mr Darcy
243/245	Elizabeth
240/257	Love and marriage

Chapter 47

245 'But why all this . . .'
What do you think of Elizabeth's assessment of Wickham's intentions? Do you think it is realistic? What does this reveal about Elizabeth's perceptiveness?

223/262	Mr Wickham
244/246	Elizabeth

246 'But why all this . . .'
Whom does Elizabeth blame for Lydia's present predicament? Look back to chapter 41, where she warned her father of possible dangers. What qualities of character does this show in Elizabeth? How do they contrast with Lydia's personality?

220/250	Lydia
245/248	Elizabeth

247 Mrs Bennet, to . . .
Notice how Mrs Bennet refuses to accept any personal responsibility for the present situation. Totally unconscious of her own shortcomings she finds others to blame for the events.

225/251	Mr and Mrs Bennet

248 Then, perceiving in . . .
What does Mary's comment about Lydia lack? Why is Elizabeth so surprised? Compare it with her own emotional response to the news of Lydia's elopement in chapter 46.

90/0	Kitty and Mary
246/249	Elizabeth

249 'Perhaps it would . . .'
Do you agree that Jane and Elizabeth 'acted with the best intentions'? Look back to chapter 40, where they discussed this matter.

213/258	Jane
248/255	Elizabeth

250 My dear Harriet, . . .
In what way does this letter confirm Lydia's character?

246/265	Lydia

251 I never saw . . .
Why would Mr Bennet be particularly shocked? What other feelings would he be experiencing at the same time, given his previous behaviour as a father?

247/253	Mr and Mrs Bennet

Chapter 48

252 All Meryton seemed . . .
Jane Austen is mocking the fickleness and superficiality of public opinion.

236/257	Social aspects
222/256	Aspects of language

Characters and ideas previous/next comment

253 Mr Gardiner left . . .

Mr Gardiner's solid character is revealed, in contrast to Mr Bennet's unreliable character. It is the former who bothers to write and inform the family of the latest moves in the search for Lydia. Mr Bennet failed in his duty to keep the family informed. As it said on the previous page he is 'a most negligent and dilatory correspondent'. Notice too, it is the uncle who takes the practical steps in trying to find Lydia.

254 I feel myself called . . .

Self-centred as ever, his letter reveals his relief at not having married into the family. It also demonstrates his total lack of heart or sense in advocating that the Bennets reject their daughter now.

255 Then, after a . . .

Notice how her father acknowledges Elizabeth's wisdom, when he admits she was right to warn him that he was not taking his paternal duties seriously enough.

256 'This is a parade,' . . .

How deeply affected is Mr Bennet? Is his flippancy due to habitual performance or does he genuinely not feel very deeply about the matter? Look how he jokes and teases Kitty on the next page. Do you think he should be blamed for being irresponsible?

Chapter 49

257 'Ten thousand pounds!' . . .

Notice the important part that money plays in marriage. Mr Bennet and Elizabeth accept that Mr Wickham would only have agreed to marry for £10,000, a vast sum in those days. Notice also how essential it was that Lydia and Wickham should marry. Even though their chance of happiness is small, and Wickham is disliked, the marriage must still go ahead because the alternative of public disgrace for Lydia and her family is so terrible.

258 'I comfort myself . . .'

As optimistic as ever about human nature, Jane feels sure Wickham must have regard for Lydia. Jane is more correct than Elizabeth in assuming that the Gardiners could not have settled that amount of money on Wickham. It is significant that Elizabeth does not suspect who is behind it.

259 'My dear, dear Lydia!' . . .

What is her first thought on hearing Lydia is to be married? Her simple mind is 'disturbed by no fear for her felicity, not humbled . . .'. Instead she thinks about the wedding clothes! Look at her ingratitude too on hearing that Mr Gardiner had given Wickham money.

Characters and ideas previous/next comment

149/0	The Gardiners
251/255	Mr and Mrs Bennet
209/292	Mr Collins
253/256	Mr and Mrs Bennet
249/258	Elizabeth
255/259	Mr and Mrs Bennet
252/270	Aspects of language
244/260	Love and marriage
252/262	Social aspects
249/277	Jane
255/260	Elizabeth
256/261	Mr and Mrs Bennet

260 Poor Lydia's situation . . .
The wisdom that Mr Bennet commented on earlier is again apparent here. In contrast to the inane prattling of her mother, Elizabeth thoughtfully assesses Lydia's situation and concludes that, while by no means idle (for she did not rate her chances of 'rational happiness nor worldly prosperity' very highly), she does see that Lydia's position is considerably better than it had been.

258/264   Elizabeth
257/264   Love and
          marriage

Chapter 50

261 Five thousand pounds . . .
He behaves in character again once the shock of Lydia's escapade has worn off. Although he is decent enough to find out the exact terms of the marriage settlement he does admit to relief that someone else is taking charge of the affair. He really is irresponsible and willing to abdicate his family duties, whenever he can.

259/263   Mr and Mrs
          Bennet

262 The good news . . .
Jane Austen mocks the public attitude to the wedding, criticizing the hypocrisy of the 'spiteful old ladies in Meryton' who, knowing what a bad character Wickham is, see little chance of Lydia being happy and yet said 'good-natured wishes for her well-doing'.

245/270   Mr Wickham
257/276   Social
          aspects

263 Her husband allowed . . .
Whom do you consider to be more correct – Mr Bennet, who wants never to see his daughter in his house again because of her behaviour, or Mrs Bennet, who totally ignores the behaviour but is scandalized that Lydia will not have the new clothes that befit a bride? Do you think Jane Austen believes either to be right? Do you? Is Mr Bennet's opinion justifiable, given his sense of responsibility in the episode?

261/273   Mr and Mrs
          Bennet

264 Elizabeth was now . . .
In the assumed knowledge that Darcy will now want nothing more to do with her, Elizabeth comes to realize fully that she and he are very well suited. Jane Austen reveals her view of the ideal marriage, one which is based on mutually suitable talents and dispositions. Elizabeth would have benefited from Darcy's knowledge of the world; Darcy from her 'ease and liveliness'. This rational approach to marriage is contrasted with Lydia and Wickham's; a marriage that Elizabeth is convinced cannot work because 'their passions were stronger than their virtue'.

244/268   Mr Darcy
260/265   Elizabeth
260/281   Love and
          marriage

Chapter 51

265 Their reception from . . .
Elizabeth, imagining how she would feel in Lydia's position, looks for signs of shame and embarrassment in Lydia's face. She is shocked to find none at all! Instead Lydia is still herself: 'untamed, unabashed, wild, noisy, fearless'.

250/266   Lydia
264/269   Elizabeth

266 'Only think of its . . .'
Lydia's insensitivity to the feelings and efforts of others who had to bring about the 'honourable' marriage is apparent in her attitude that it would be 'fun' to be married. Her behaviour is as gauche and insensitive as her mother's. Look at the way she let William Goulding know she was married, or the way she talks to Jane.

265/267   Lydia

267 'La! You are . . .'
Totally immune to sense or advice, notice what she is doing while Mrs Gardiner is trying to talk to her on the morning of her wedding.

266/0   Lydia

Chapter 52

268 I have just received . . .
Darcy stresses that he feels it is his fault that Wickham has been misunderstood and for that reason he is providing the money so that the marriage may take place. Mrs Gardiner believes he is also doing it for another reason. What could this be?

264/269   Mr Darcy

269 The contents of . . .
Elizabeth, conscious that Darcy has acted as much because of her as for any other reason, regrets all the 'saucy speech' and the 'ungracious sensation' she had towards him. She admits her love for him but is not ready to admit that he wants to marry her as she is sure that he would not want Wickham for a brother-in-law.

268/274   Mr Darcy
265/270   Elizabeth

270 'That you were . . .'
In a very subtle and ironic way Elizabeth lets Wickham know that she is aware of the truth about him. Look how she lets it be known that the housekeeper has given a true picture of him. Even if Elizabeth pretends that she has not necessarily believed it, Wickham must know she is being ironic.

262/271   Mr Wickham
269/271   Elizabeth
256/272   Aspects of
          language

271 'I dare say she . . .'
Irony is used most pointedly here. Elizabeth suggests to Wickham that she knows about his planned elopement with Darcy's sister, too, when she says 'she has got over the most trying age'.

270/272   Mr Wickham
270/276   Elizabeth

Chapter 53

272 Mr Wickham was so . . .
Jane Austen is being ironic in the opening sentence of this paragraph. Elizabeth has made it known to him, very subtly, that she knows all about his past so he is quite willing (even satisfied!) not to bring up the subject again in conversation.

271/0   Mr Wickham
270/295   Aspects of
          language

273 'Well, well, and . . .'
In her usual inconsistent, insensitive way she rattles on about Bingley's arrival, having said she will not talk about it and having no consideration at all for Jane's feelings.

263/275	Mr and Mrs Bennet

274 Darcy, after enquiring . . .
Darcy seems to have reverted to his former manner. To what does Elizabeth attribute his thoughtful and silent behaviour?

269/278	Mr Darcy

275 'I began to be . . .'
Unwittingly increasing Elizabeth's embarrassment, Mrs Bennet talks without shame about the wedding and, awkwardly for Elizabeth, about Wickham.

273/285	Mr and Mrs Bennet

276 Elizabeth, who knew . . .
Elizabeth is filled with despair by the insensitivity of her mother and feels that, even if Bingley and Darcy are fond of Jane and her, the same lack of breeding on Mrs Bennet's part which caused the problems previously, will cause them once again.

271/278	Elizabeth
262/284	Social aspects

277 Yet the misery . . .
Elizabeth's pessimism is not so deeply founded as she feared, for she becomes aware of an awakening of interest in Bingley towards Jane.

238/279	Mr Bingley
258/279	Jane

Chapter 54

278 Darcy had walked . . .
The suspense about Elizabeth and Darcy is prolonged by Darcy's quiet, distant behaviour. Elizabeth is kept on tenterhooks, unsure if he will want to marry or not, understanding that it would be beneath the pride of any man to ask the same woman twice.

274/291	Mr Darcy
276/279	Elizabeth

279 'You are very . . .'
This part of the story is developing well, with everyone except Jane sure of the growing affection between herself and Bingley. Elizabeth, in her usual sceptical way, refuses to believe Jane's protestations.

277/280	Mr Bingley
277/281	Jane
278/283	Elizabeth

Chapter 55

280 Mrs Bennet's schemes . . .
Level-headed and even-tempered, look how well he tolerates Mrs Bennet.

279/281	Mr Bingley

281 He then shut . . .
Jane Austen's ideal of marriage is set out here. Happiness is 'rationally founded', and marriage is likely to happen between Jane and Bingley because of their 'excellent understanding' and 'a general similarity of feeling and taste' between the two.

280/282	Mr Bingley
279/282	Jane
264/295	Love and marriage

| | | Characters and ideas previous/next comment |

282 'You are a . . .'

How true is Mr Bennet's assessment of Jane's and Bingley's characters? You must be able to refer to events of the novel to support your answer.

| 281/0 | Mr Bingley |
| 281/0 | Jane |

283 'If you were . . .'

Notice that Elizabeth, even though despondent about Darcy, can, because of her happiness for her sister, make jokes about her own spinsterhood.

| 279/286 | Elizabeth |

284 The situation of . . .

Here, the author is satirizing the fickleness of public opinion.

| 276/288 | Social aspects |

Chapter 56

285 'You have a very . . .'

Notice the extremely hurtful way Lady de Bourgh criticizes the house and garden. Notice how Mrs Bennet, overwhelmed by the presence of such an illustrious person, is civil to her, despite her ladyship's rudeness.

| 275/293 | Mr and Mrs Bennet |
| 206/286 | Lady Catherine |

286 'Your ladyship has . . .'

Elizabeth, refusing to be intimidated by rank and already incensed at Lady de Bourgh's offensive manner, resists answering her questions directly. She feels very strongly that this woman is not entitled to know her business.

| 285/287 | Lady Catherine |
| 283/287 | Elizabeth |

287 'Let us sit . . .'

Imagine what a shock Elizabeth's defiance must be to Lady de Bourgh because, as she says, 'I have not been used to submit . . . I have not been in the habit of . . .'.

| 286/288 | Lady Catherine |
| 286/289 | Elizabeth |

288 'I will not be . . .'

Lady de Bourgh makes it plain that for class reasons she is against a marriage between Darcy and Elizabeth: 'The upstart pretensions of a young woman without family, connection or fortune'.

| 287/290 | Lady Catherine |
| 284/0 | Social aspects |

289 'And I certainly . . .'

Notice the intensely reasonable line of argument that Elizabeth takes. Of course she is right to say that if she refused Darcy's proposal then that would not mean he would propose to Miss de Bourgh or that she would accept. Notice too the personal dignity with which she responds to this interfering woman, who intimidates most people.

| 287/290 | Elizabeth |

290 'You can *now* . . .'

Even when Lady de Bourgh stoops to the lowest and flings the Lydia/Wickham accusation at her (one that would have hit home, too, for she has voiced this fear herself) Elizabeth musters all her dignity and cuts the conversation dead. Notice it is Elizabeth and not Lady Catherine who brings the conversation to a halt.

| 280/0 | Lady Catherine |
| 289/291 | Elizabeth |

Chapter 57

291 In revolving lady . . .
We are still kept in suspense about the outcome of the friendship between Elizabeth and Darcy. She is unsure of his feelings and imagines the worst outcome of her interview with Darcy's aunt.

previous/next	comment
278/295	Mr Darcy
290/294	Elizabeth
238/294	Structure

292 After mentioning the . . .'
What does Mr Collin's letter reveal about his character? Do you think it is the kind of letter that a clergyman should write?

previous/next	comment
254/0	Mr Collins

293 'Yes – *that* is . . .'
Mr Bennet's sense of the absurd is aroused by the suggestion that Darcy is interested in Elizabeth for he still thinks that she loathes him. The impossibility of such a match strikes him as amusing. He does not realize how hurtful he is being to his daughter.

previous/next	comment
285/301	Mr and Mrs Bennet

294 To this question . . .
We are left at the end of the chapter sympathizing with Elizabeth who is unsure of Darcy's feelings towards her. The suspense is kept up as her doubts are renewed. She has to admit the possibility that her father is right and that she is wrong about Darcy.

previous/next	comment
291/295	Elizabeth
291/296	Structure

Chapter 58

295 Elizabeth was too . . .
Look at the way Jane Austen treats the declaration of love. The emphasis is on words; there is no physical contact between the lovers. Elizabeth could not even see Darcy's face as he declares his love. All emotion comes through the voice. Jane Austen rates highly the importance of conversation as the basis of a good relationship.

previous/next	comment
291/297	Mr Darcy
294/296	Elizabeth
281/0	Love and marriage
272/0	Aspects of language

296 She explained what . . .
Jane Austen is neatly tying all the ends. Elizabeth carefully relates how 'her former prejudices had been removed'.

previous/next	comment
295/298	Elizabeth
232/0	Prejudice
294/297	Structure

297 'I cannot give . . .'
The ends are tied in regard to Darcy's behaviour. He says, 'By you, I was properly humbled'. So his pride, too, has disappeared.

previous/next	comment
295/298	Mr Darcy
237/0	Pride
296/0	Structure

298 Elizabeth longed to . . .
Although they have resolved all their difficulties, Elizabeth is sensitive enough to appreciate that they have still to grow closer together. Though she realizes that she will make a good foil to his serious nature with her witty, spirited repartee, she knows that he is still not ready to be teased.

previous/next	comment
297/300	Mr Darcy
296/299	Elizabeth

Characters and ideas previous/next comment

Chapter 59

299 The evening passed . . .
Not quite all the knots have been untied because Elizabeth is uneasy about her family's reaction to the news. Therefore she cannot allow her happiness to overflow. Note the emphasis again of control of feelings by rational means.

300 'It has been . . .'
What do you think of Elizabeth's reply? Does this show a materialistic streak?

301 He then recollected . . .
Mr Bennet cannot resist the quip, seeing the humour in everything. What is he insinuating here?

302 'Good gracious! . . .'
What is her reaction to the news of the marriage? Is she concerned that she dislikes the man? What strikes her first? 'Tis as good as a Lord', she remarks.

Characters and ideas	
previous/next comment	
298/300	Elizabeth
298/302	Mr Darcy
299/0	Elizabeth
293/302	Mr and Mrs Bennet
301/0	Mr and Mrs Bennet
300/0	Mr Darcy

Characters in the novel

This is a very brief overview of each character. You should use it as a starting point for your own studies of characterization. For each of the aspects of character mentioned you should look in your text for evidence to support or contradict the views expressed here, and indeed, your own views as well.

Know the incidents and conversations which will support and enlarge upon your knowledge of each character. You will find it helpful to select a character and follow the commentary, referring always to the text to read and digest the context of the comment.

Mr Bennet

Mr Bennet is an intelligent, witty man who nevertheless fails in his duty as a father. Disillusioned by an unhappy marriage, he retreats from his family, physically by taking refuge in his library and morally by refusing to take seriously the responsibility of parenthood. Instead of guiding and teaching his daughters he teases and mocks them. Although shocked and chastened by Lydia's elopement his character does not really change. He leaves it to others to sort out the trouble as he reverts to his lazy and selfish life.

Mrs Bennet

Mrs Bennet is a woman of little intelligence or understanding. She is insensitive to the feelings of others, superficial in thought, loud in speech. She is an embarrassment to her husband and Elizabeth. Her main preoccupation is to see her five daughters married. This desire dominates all other considerations. The morality of Lydia's behaviour is of no importance to her once the wedding has been announced. Her sole thought is of the clothes Lydia will need. She is a woman of superficial feeling, quickly irritated but equally rapidly calmed. Her opinion of Darcy changes immediately on hearing that he is to marry Elizabeth. She is childish in her judgment of people, blaming Mr Collins for the entailment and Bingley for Jane's unhappiness. She is the butt of her husband's sarcasm. Ironically it is her lack of breeding that almost prevents Jane and Elizabeth from making their satisfactory matches.

Elizabeth Bennet

Elizabeth, the second of the Bennet daughters and her father's favourite, is the heroine of the novel. She is intelligent, lively, witty and quite capable of holding her own in conversation with someone as well educated as Darcy. She is a strong character with sufficient belief in herself to stand up to such figures as Mr Collins, Lady de Bourgh and Darcy. She is deeply affectionate as witnessed by the sorrow she feels for Jane, whose compassionate nature she much admires. She is perceptive, which helps her to assess accurately the characters of Bingley, his sister and Lady de Bourgh, but is wrong when she judges Wickham and Darcy. Completely taken in by appearances she unquestioningly accepts all that Wickham says. She is proud, however, and it is her hurt pride that first makes her prejudiced against Darcy. It is her pride, too, that is flattered by Wickham, who singles her out for personal attention. It is this mixture of pride and prejudice that blunts her judgment of the two men.

Elizabeth reveals a maturity and wisdom that is above her parents. She censures her father for not acting more responsibly towards his children. She finds her mother's preoccupation with trivia irksome. The atmosphere at home is too confining for her spirits.

Above all else, it is Elizabeth's teasing, impulsive, cheerful disposition, which makes her so appealing. As Darcy says near the end, it was the 'liveliness of' her 'mind' that first attracted him.

Jane Bennet

Jane is the eldest daughter and the most beautiful. She is a sweet-natured girl whose only fault is her desire to find good in everyone. This leads her sometimes to be undiscerning in her assessment of character. She refuses for a long time to believe that Miss Bingley is being hypocritical. She tries to see virtue in both Wickham and Darcy at the same time. She is an excellent foil to Elizabeth, slowing down the latter's often hasty conclusions about people. Their affectionate relationship is one of the most pleasing aspects of the book. Jane keeps her own feelings hidden and while this helps her to cope when Bingley is away, it did also lead Darcy into believing that she did not care very much for Bingley in the first place. Jane, although a very pleasant character, is naïve. It is no surprise to find that she and her equally 'compliant' husband, Bingley, move to be nearer Elizabeth and Darcy, who are, after all, the strongest characters.

Kitty Bennet

Catherine, known as Kitty, Bennet is very much under the influence of Lydia, who is more extrovert. She follows her younger sister and enjoys the same pursuits. Unable to go to Brighton she is perhaps saved from a similar fate as Lydia. Their experience with their youngest daughter makes Mr and Mrs Bennet take a firmer hand with Kitty, and under the influence of her elder sisters she becomes 'less irritable, less ignorant and less insipid'.

Lydia Bennet

Lydia is the youngest Bennet daughter and the first to be married as she so proudly announces. Very much like her mother she is self-centred, frivolous, superficial, interested only in clothes, dances and the neighbouring officers. She is shameless about her behaviour with Wickham and quite unaware of the anxiety and trouble she has caused her family. She is unfeeling and tactless, especially to her sisters after her marriage. Elizabeth is very critical of her, considering her 'ignorant, idle and vain'.

Mary Bennet

She is the most studious of the Bennet girls, although not the most intelligent. Her comments are learnèd but they lack the wit of Elizabeth or the compassion of Jane. Once out of the shadow of her two more gifted sisters she does become more sociable.

Caroline Bingley

Miss Bingley is rich, proud and very aware of her social position. She scorns the Bennet family for their lack of sophistication and because they have relations in 'trade'. The irony is that it is this source that created her inherited wealth! Although superficially civil she especially despises Elizabeth as she is jealous of the attention that Darcy pays her. Miss Bingley speaks very spitefully and sarcastically about Elizabeth in a vain attempt to gain Darcy's interest herself. Although one may feel sorry for her in that she is unable to attract the man she wants, she remains nonetheless a hypocrite and a snob.

Charles Bingley

Charles Bingley is a rich, handsome, eligible young man who rents a house three miles away from the Bennets' home. He is very sociable, uncomplicated and agreeable. Unlike his sister or his friend, Darcy, he is not offended by the Bennet family's lack of breeding. He is very attracted to Jane, but being of a compliant disposition, he is easily persuaded by his sister and his friend to leave the neighbourhood and return to London.

Lady Catherine de Bourgh

Lady Catherine de Bourgh has an overdeveloped sense of her own importance. She feels that her rank as a Lady gives her leave to offer opinions to anyone and everyone on any subject at all. She is not in the habit of being contradicted. With people like Mr Collins about, to offer flattery freely and to obey her every command, she is indeed unused to disagreement. Her habit of speaking her mind is no excuse for incivility, and it is ironic that Darcy has to feel embarassed for his aunt's lack of breeding when she is so bad-mannered to Elizabeth. So used is she to having her own way that she is taken completely by surprise when Elizabeth rejects her advice not to marry Darcy.

Mr Collins

Mr Collins is a figure greatly satirized by Jane Austen because he is pompous, insensitive and a fool. Obsequious to Lady de Bourgh, he is not perceptive enough to see that she is patronizing him. His lack of self-knowledge and his uncritical mind mean that he does not understand why Elizabeth rejects him. Although his pride is hurt by such a rejection, his feelings are shallow for he changes to Charlotte Lucas almost immediately. His materialistic outlook on life, which makes him value the quantity or size of houses and furnishings while totally ignoring their aesthetic quality, ill-befits a clergyman even of those days. His lack of Christian spirit is revealed in the letter he sends the Bennets after Lydia's marriage.

Darcy

The difficulty in assessing Fitzwilliam Darcy's character is that he is seen almost entirely through Elizabeth's eyes. Therefore it is necessary to look behind her prejudice to find the true man. Certainly, on first meeting he is proud and unnecessarily rude about Elizabeth. However, it is soon apparent to the reader that his first impressions of her were wrong and he becomes increasingly attracted to her. He attributes his haughtiness and lack of ease in public to shyness. 'We neither of us perform well to strangers', he says to Elizabeth. Shy or not, he does not tolerate other people well. Unlike Bingley, who is his opposite in character, he finds Mrs Bennet's behaviour vulgar and embarrassing. Elizabeth's inferior background concerns him for a long time. He has a cutting wit which puts people in their place when he feels they have overstepped the bounds of decorum. Both Miss Bingley and Sir William Lucas feel the edge of his tongue.

His good qualities remain hidden until Elizabeth goes to Pemberley. There she learns what a fine master, landlord and brother he is. He, in his turn, chastened by Elizabeth's rebuff at Hunsford, modifies his behaviour, accepting that he did act with pride in proposing in the way that he did. The full extent of Darcy's good nature is revealed in his treatment of the Wickham-Lydia affair. His generosity to them is enormous and his sense of responsibility admirable. Although a more humbled person at the end, he still remains serious. Elizabeth knows that he is not ready to be teased although she has every intention of making him less serious with her 'lively, sportive manner of talking'.

Colonel Fitzwilliam

Darcy's cousin is a pleasant, sociable man. His role in the plot is more important than his character. He helps Darcy clarify his feelings towards Elizabeth. Darcy is jealous of the ease with which his cousin and Elizabeth talk together and is thus able to measure his own affection for Elizabeth. Colonel Fitzwilliam is able to show Darcy off in a better light and to explain Darcy's character a little better. His main function is, however, to provide Elizabeth with information that will have an important effect on the development of the plot. He lets it be known to her that Darcy did know of Jane's whereabouts in London but kept it from Bingley. Thus Elizabeth's anger at Darcy is at its highest point when he makes his proposal. A refusal is absolutely guaranteed.

The Gardiners

Mr and Mrs Gardiner, Elizabeth's aunt and uncle, come from London. Although they have only made their living in 'trade', they are well-educated, well-bred people who can hold their own in any company. The proof of this is when they meet Darcy. He is very impressed by their 'civility'. Mr Gardiner, with his basic common sense, is the man who sorts out the mess of Lydia's elopement. Mrs Gardiner is a good friend and aunt to Elizabeth offering advice about the danger of romantic love. Darcy has much to be grateful for to them both, as it was they who took Elizabeth to Derbyshire.

The Lucases

The Lucases are friends of the Bennets. Mr Lucas has been made a knight and his new status quite overwhelms him. Although a pleasant, well-meaning fellow, he is always self-consciously obsequious in superior company. He is flattering to Mr Darcy and Lady de Bourgh in a way that makes him the butt of Jane Austen's satire.

Charlotte Lucas

Charlotte, Elizabeth's friend, is a realist. Aware of her poor financial status, she is prepared to marry solely for economic reasons. Although this attitude shocks Elizabeth, there were very few options open to a woman in her position. Having made the decision to become mistress of Hunsford, Mr Collins's home, she carries out her duties correctly and amiably and seems happy. She is sensible to realize that she must keep on good terms with Lady de Bourgh, so she pays the necessary courtesy visits and avoids confrontation. She cleverly reorganizes the rooms at Hunsford to ensure that she sees little enough of Mr Collins during the day!

George Wickham

George Wickham, an officer in the regiment stationed at Meryton, near Longbourn, is an attractive figure who deceives Elizabeth, her family and the neighbourhood into thinking that he is a worthy character. His story about the injustice he has suffered at the hand of Darcy is sufficient to draw everyone's sympathy and approval. No one stops to check the truth of his story. His is accepted uncritically. Elizabeth even excuses his mercenary reasons for changing his interest from her to Miss King. His true character is only revealed by Darcy under pressure. Wickham is a spendthrift, a liar, a womanizer. He can only be persuaded to marry Lydia, and so stop a dreadful scandal, by being given a great sum of money by Darcy. Marriage does not change him: he is constantly in debt.

What happens in each chapter

Chapter 1 The arrival of Mr Bingley at Netherfield Park is keenly anticipated by Mrs Bennet, whose main purpose in life is to see her five daughters successfully married. Her husband does not share her excitement and is unhelpful and contemptuous of her efforts. He demonstrates a distinct lack of interest in family affairs.

Chapter 2 Mr Bennet enjoys teasing his family by keeping them ignorant of his visit to Netherfield Hall. Mrs Bennet is irritated by this hitch in her plans, but her mood soon turns to joy when Mr Bennet reveals that he has visited Mr Bingley.

Chapter 3 Mr Bingley returns Mr Bennet's visit, but the ladies, not seeing more than a glimpse of him, have to be content with secondhand information about him, until they go to the ball he holds at Netherfield Hall. Here the opinion that Mr Bingley is agreeable and handsome is confirmed but, in contrast, his friend Mr Darcy is found to be proud and unfriendly. He offends Mrs Bennet deeply by slighting Elizabeth, but she, unlike her mother, does not take his comments to heart. Mrs Bennet is gratified that Jane seems to have made a good impression on Mr Bingley.

Chapter 4 This chapter involves the four main characters of the book. Jane and Elizabeth are seen in contrast, as are Bingley and Darcy. Jane reveals a kind, uncritical nature, ready to see only good in people. Elizabeth is more intelligent, more observant, and more ready to see through people's actions. She is less impressed by Bingley's sisters than Jane. They have had all the privilege and upbringing of ladies and should therefore act as such. Elizabeth is sceptical that they do. Bingley and Darcy are seen as opposites: the former, less clever, but more agreeable and sociable; the latter 'haughty and reserved'. Their opinions of the ball are very different.

Chapter 5 The Bennets discuss the ball with their friends, the Lucases. Mrs Bennet is delighted with Jane's success at having danced twice with Bingley. Everyone except Jane is agreed that Darcy's character is quite unpleasant and that his pride is overbearing. Only Charlotte Lucas feels that his social rank gives him the right to be proud.

Chapter 6 The acquaintance between the Bingleys and the Bennets grows and although the former admit to liking Jane and Elizabeth the rest of the family are found to be 'intolerable'. Elizabeth's liking for them, however, does not grow. Charlotte Lucas warns that Jane must make her feelings clear if she wishes to encourage Bingley. Her scheming, cynical view of marriage, whereby a woman may as well marry for money as love, as 'marriage is entirely a matter of chance', contradicts Elizabeth's view that marriage must be based on mutual knowledge and understanding. Elizabeth becomes aware that Darcy is taking a keener interest in her. Through pride she refuses to dance with him, as she assumes he is merely being polite. Miss Bingley is surprised that Darcy seems to have changed his opinion of Elizabeth, and she immediately appears jealous.

Chapter 7 Mrs Bennet's eagerness to see her daughters married is explained. Mr Bennet's estate will not be left to them on his death, and therefore for economic reasons they need to marry well. The younger daughters are delighted at the arrival of a militia regiment in Meryton and Mrs Bennet approves of their association with the officers. Jane receives an invitation to dine at Netherfield and Mrs Bennet works out a ruse to enable her to spend the night there. The plan goes amiss as Jane becomes ill and has to stay there in bed. Elizabeth goes to look after her. Thus Jane Austen has brought her four main characters under one roof in order that they might become better acquainted.

Chapter 8   The Bingley sisters' concern for Jane is superficial. They also are very critical of Elizabeth when she is out of the room. They are scornful of the Bennets' social rank. Miss Bingley attempts to impress Mr Darcy with compliments and praise, but it is Elizabeth's intelligence and independence of thought which he notices.

Jane's health continues to give cause for concern.

Chapter 9   Mrs Bennet arrives to see Jane. Having assured herself of Jane's recovery, she is happy to converse with the occupants of Netherfield. Much to the discomfort of her daughter, Elizabeth, she shows herself to be inquisitive, insulting, shallow, and narrow-minded. Elizabeth, in contrast, is witty and intelligent and impresses Darcy further. He is left with the problem of liking the daughter but scorning the mother. Mr Bingley promises Lydia that he will hold a ball when Jane is better.

Chapter 10   Miss Bingley flatters and compliments Mr Darcy but with little effect. Mr Bingley, Mr Darcy and Elizabeth engage in a discussion about Bingley's hastiness and willingness to agree with his friends. Mr Darcy and Elizabeth match each other in intelligence and witty repartee. Darcy's interest in Elizabeth grows but she, still prejudiced against him, senses only disapproval in his regard to her. Miss Bingley, out of jealousy, is very spiteful and sarcastic about the Bennet family.

Chapter 11   Jane is better and joins the rest of the company in the drawing room. Miss Bingley tries unsuccessfully to distract Darcy from his reading, until she persuades Elizabeth to accompany her on a walk round the room. Then he looks up. In the ensuing conversation, Elizabeth reveals her pleasure in laughing at the absurdities of human behaviour. Darcy admits his dislike of being mocked and claims to conduct himself in a way that will not invite ridicule. Elizabeth teases him about this very self-conscious and serious side of his character. Darcy, sensing his growing attraction to Elizabeth, brings the conversation to a halt but not before he has admitted Elizabeth's prejudice against him.

Chapter 12   This chapter acts as an interlude between the sojourn at Netherfield and the arrival of Mr Collins at Longbourn. The interval at Netherfield has enabled the four chief characters to be better acquainted. Mr Darcy is glad of the subsequent separation as he is not yet willing to submit to his growing love for Elizabeth. The girls are welcomed home, especially by their father, as he has missed their enlivening company.

Chapter 13   Mr Bennet announces the imminent arrival of a stranger. He shows his family the letter that has preceded Mr Collins. He is the distant cousin who stands to inherit the Bennet estate. He is a clergyman, who has a living on the estate of a Lady Catherine de Bourgh. On meeting him he proves to be as pompous as his letter suggests. He says that he would like to help the family, and hints that he is willing to marry one of the daughters, as he comes 'prepared to admire them'.

Chapter 14   Much to the amusement of Mr Bennet, Mr Collins reveals what a fool he is in accepting and, even more so, being grateful for the attention of Lady de Bourgh and her daughter. He fails to see that he is being patronized by them, but he bathes in the glory of their attention, convinced that their rank itself gives them grounds to be admired. Mr Bennet sees Mr Collins as an absurd figure, laying himself open to ridicule through his pomposity and blind deference to Lady de Bourgh. Interestingly, Mrs Bennet accepts Mr Collins at face value, and quite approves of him. The younger daughters have no time for his seriousness, preferring to talk about the officers than listen to him reading sermons.

Chapter 15   Mr Collins reveals an amazing superficiality in the way he can swing his feelings so rapidly from Jane to Elizabeth.

The girls meet Wickham for the first time and they are favourably impressed by his 'gentlemanlike appearance'. There is an air of mystery about Wickham and Darcy which Elizabeth quickly discerns. Mr Collins and Mrs Philips are satirized for their mutual admiration which is based on nothing deeper than exaggerated civilities.

Chapter 16   At a gathering at Mrs Philips's house, Elizabeth meets Wickham again. Taken in by his agreeable appearance she listens in astonishment to his misfortunes. Wickham tells her that his father had once been the loyal and trusted employee of Darcy's father. Consequently Wickham had been treated like a second son and had been led to understand that a clerical living would be his one day. When the living became vacant Darcy broke his father's promise and refused to give it to Wickham. Wickham attributes this dishonourable behaviour to jealousy and proceeds to blacken Darcy's name and character. Elizabeth, because of her prejudice against Darcy and her attraction towards Wickham, believes him even though she has no proof.

Chapter 17   Jane, on hearing Wickham's story from Elizabeth, refuses to condemn Darcy, suggesting that the full account has not yet been known. Elizabeth, completely taken in by Wickham, is convinced that it is true.

Bingley and his two sisters pass by with invitations for the ball at Netherfield. The sisters are anxious to leave before they have to meet Mrs Bennet. The five girls greet the news of the ball in their own individual ways, and spend the next few days planning for it. Elizabeth is looking forward to dancing with Wickham but Mr Collins informs her of his intention to dance with her. She begins to realize that it is she who has been singled out as his prospective wife.

Chapter 18   The first disappointment of the ball, for Elizabeth, is the absence of Wickham. The second is the dances with Mr Collins, which are miserable affairs. Mr Darcy takes her by surprise and she dances with him. Unable to learn much from him about Wickham, she clings to her belief in his story and will not be persuaded against it even by the contrary evidence of Miss Bingley or her sister Jane. She is further shamed by her family who each in their turn makes fools of themselves – Collins by introducing himself to Darcy; her mother by talking loudly about hopes of a marriage between Bingley and Jane; and Mary by singing. The evening upsets her completely and it ends with her having to endure Mr Collins's constant attention. The final embarrassment is Mrs Bennet's deliberate ploy to leave last, when it is obvious to Elizabeth that they have overstayed their welcome; Mrs Bennet with her usual lack of perception is quite unaware of this.

Chapter 19   Mr Collins declares his intention to propose to Elizabeth, and Mrs Bennet consents. His proposal consists of a list of reasons why he needs to marry. They are a desire to set an example, because he feels it will add to his happiness, because Lady de Bourgh has suggested it and finally he has chosen a Bennet to recompense in some way for taking the inheritance from the daughters. Elizabeth refuses his offer but he will not accept the refusal, believing that it is feminine wile on her part. She is still determined even after he reminds her that a woman in her poor economic position may not ever receive another offer.

Chapter 20   Mrs Bennet is shocked to hear that her daughter has refused Mr Collins's proposal and she begs her husband to talk to Elizabeth. To Mrs Bennet's surprise, far from trying to persuade his daughter, he is absolutely against the marriage. Behind Mrs Bennet's disappointment is a real worry about Elizabeth's future should Mr Bennet die before her daughter's marriage. In his usual unctuous manner, Mr Collins renounces the pursuit of Elizabeth.

Chapter 21   Mr Collins treats the matter of the turned down proposal with 'resentful silence'. Elizabeth meets Wickham again, who explains that he stayed away from the ball because he did not want to meet Darcy. Elizabeth is complimented by his attention. A letter from Caroline Bingley reveals the departure of the Bingley family to London. Jane takes all she says at face value and is hurt by her suggestion that Bingley could become interested in Darcy's sister. Elizabeth, as perspicacious as ever, sees most of the letter as wishful thinking on Caroline's part. Miss Bingley hopes that her brother will become interested in Georgiana Darcy to make the path easier for her approach to Darcy himself. Elizabeth is still confident of Bingley's affection for Jane.

Chapter 22   Charlotte Lucas entertains Mr Collins after his failure with Elizabeth, and he quickly turns his attention to her. Unlike Elizabeth, Charlotte is happy to accept his proposal, not because she loves him, in fact she finds him irksome, but because he offers her the financial security she wants. Her family is delighted with the prospect of her one day being mistress of Longbourn. Elizabeth is upset that she should mary for economic reasons.

Chapter 23   Sir William goes to Longbourn to break the news of his daughter's engagement, where it is received with much incivility. Mrs Bennet is very angry that her family has lost such an eligible man and relations between the Lucases and the Bennets become strained. Even the friendship between Elizabeth and Charlotte cools. Mr Collins writes of his imminent return to Longbourn but he will find a cool reception waiting him. In her mood of despondency, Bingley's silence leads Elizabeth to suspect that her worst fears will come true, and his sisters will have succeeded in keeping him in London all winter.

Chapter 24   Their fears that Mr Bingley will stay in London are confirmed. The reaction of Jane and Elizabeth to this news typifies the difference in character between the two girls. Jane, although upset, accepts the news, and wonders if she might have been wrong in her assumption that Bingley's sisters have successfully persuaded their compliant brother to stay away deliberately. Elizabeth reveals her high ideals of marriage, and criticizes her friend Charlotte Lucas for her practical view on marriage. Mr Bennet reacts to Jane's plight with his usual flippancy, and it is left to Mr Wickham to cheer up the family. He is regarded with favour, especially as his popularity feeds the opinion that Darcy is a dislikeable man.

Chapter 25   Mr Collins leaves, and Mr and Mrs Gardiner, Elizabeth's aunt and uncle, arrive from London. Although only in trade, they are a sensible, lively, intelligent couple, particularly liked by Jane and Elizabeth. On hearing of Jane's situation, Mrs Gardiner invites her to return to London with them. The possibility of her meeting with Bingley is doubted by Elizabeth as the social gulf between the two families is so great. Mrs Gardiner joins in the general prejudice against Darcy.

Chapter 26   Mrs Gardiner warns Elizabeth to show caution in her affections towards Wickham because of his lack of fortune. Mr Collins returns to Longbourn and the marriage takes place between Charlotte Lucas and him. Jane meets Miss Bingley in London and is finally convinced of her deceit in keeping Jane's whereabouts hidden from her brother. Elizabeth is glad that Jane can see the situation clearly. Wickham turns his attention from Elizabeth to Miss King, a wealthy woman and it is a sign of her lack of concern for him that Elizabeth understands and does not censure his mercenary values.

Chapter 27   Elizabeth goes with Sir William Lucas to Hunsford to visit Charlotte. En route they spend time in London with the Gardiners. She learns that Jane is still upset about Bingley. Elizabeth too is in low spirits and in need of a change. The Gardiners propose that she visits the Lakes with them in the summer.

Chapter 28   Elizabeth arrives at Hunsford more cheerful after a day's journey, and happier in the knowledge of her sister's good health and the prospective journey north. Mr Collins, whom she sees has not been changed by marriage, is still pedantic and pompous. Charlotte, too, seems content and unaffected by her marriage to him. The next day, amidst great pandemonium, she learns that Miss de Bourgh has stopped outside. Elizabeth is not impressed by her and is faintly pleased that she will do quite well for Darcy.

Chapter 29   The party from Hunsford visits Rosings the next day to meet Lady de Bourgh. She is as haughty as portrayed previously and all, except Elizabeth, are in awe of her. Conscious of her superior rank, Lady de Bourgh feels it gives her the right to offer advice even on domestic matters and to ask all manner of impertinent questions. Elizabeth stands up to her and senses that she may be the first person ever to have done so. Elizabeth is not impressed by her but keeps her feelings to herself for the sake of Charlotte.

Chapter 30   Sir William Lucas leaves Hunsford and Elizabeth settles in there to a quiet routine of talking to Charlotte and walking in the grounds. They are not often bothered by Mr Collins who spends much of his time either at Rosings or alone in his book room. Two weeks pass and they learn that Mr Darcy and his cousin Colonel Fitzwilliam have come to stay with their aunt at Rosings. Both gentlemen come immediately to pay their compliments to the Collinses and Elizabeth. Elizabeth cannot resist mentioning that

Jane has been in London for three months. Mr Darcy looks uncomfortable when he admits that he has not seen her there.

Chapter 31   A belated invitation to meet Darcy and Colonel Fitzwilliam arrives. Elizabeth finds the company of the latter enjoyable, a fact that does not go unnoticed by Darcy. His aunt speaks tactlessly to Elizabeth and Darcy is obviously embarassed. In a witty exchange between Elizabeth, Darcy and Colonel Fitzwilliam, Darcy's lack of social grace is discussed. He protests that his bad manners are due to shyness not pride. It is apparent that the bond between Darcy and Elizabeth is growing, although Elizabeth still fails to sense this.

Chapter 32   To Elizabeth's surprise Darcy arrived unannounced at Hunsford. They talk with the Collinses and argue about the significance of distance. Darcy is struck by Elizabeth's unparochial character and many visits follow, the reasons for which remain unclear to Elizabeth. Darcy's interest in her is apparent, however, to the reader, and the tension increases as the plot moves towards the climax.

Chapter 33   The 'chance' meetings between Elizabeth and Darcy become more frequent. Elizabeth, still blind in her prejudice against Darcy, sees no design behind them. Elizabeth learns through Colonel Fitzwilliam that Darcy is chiefly responsible for Bingley's failure to return to Netherfield, and she, in her indignation, attributes Darcy's action to his pride. Elizabeth is now at the height of her dislike for Darcy and will not receive his proposal in a receptive frame of mind.

Chapter 34   At the height of Elizabeth's indignation towards him, Darcy arrives and proposes marriage, clearly certain that he will be accepted. Elizabeth is angered by his pompous self-assurance and does not hide her reasons for declining the proposal. He has spoiled her sister's happiness, caused Wickham's state of poverty, as well as having a pride that has repelled her from the beginning. Darcy is stunned by her answer as well as the accusation that he should have behaved in 'a more gentleman-like manner'. He leaves abruptly, and Elizabeth reminds herself of all his faults, conscious of the significance of her action in turning down such an eligible man as Darcy.

Chapter 35   Darcy gives Elizabeth a letter in which he seeks to explain himself on two accounts. Firstly, he says why he persuaded Bingley to stay in London for the winter. Convinced of Bingley's regard for Jane, he was unsure that Jane returned this affection. Darcy is prepared to admit that he may have been wrong about Jane's feelings for Bingley. Secondly, he explains his version of the Wickham story. His account tallies with Wickham's in respect of the relationship between their fathers. Also he agrees that a living was to be made available to Wickham if he took holy orders. But, and here the two accounts differ, Wickham asked for money in lieu of the living and a sum of three thousand pounds was settled on him. Darcy then goes on to explain how, when Wickham had frittered away the money, he came back demanding his right to the living. This Darcy refused to give him. The final surprise of the letter was the news of Wickham's attempt to elope with Darcy's sister, in order to gain access to her large fortune. Darcy finished the letter by asking Elizabeth to refer to Colonel Fitzwilliam if she wanted to corroborate his story.

Chapter 36   This chapter is the turning point in Elizabeth's attitude to Darcy. The realization comes to her after constantly rereading his letter that 'she had been blind, partial, prejudiced, absurd'. She accepts that she has taken Wickham's story on face value without any prior knowledge of his character or background. Only now does she apply the 'discernment' upon which she prides herself and acknowledges that Wickham's conduct was that of a coward and an insincere man, who was willing to defame Darcy's character even when he said he would not. Reluctantly she has to admit that in his behaviour Darcy could never have been accused of being unjust or unprincipled. She even has to acknowledge that Jane had not revealed her feelings to Bingley, and her family was guilty of all that Darcy accused them.

Chapter 37   Elizabeth prepares to travel home and refuses to accept Lady Catherine's suggestion that she should stay longer. She ponders long over Darcy's letter and although admits to feeling gratitude and respect for him, has not yet learnt to like or love him. She sadly concludes that it is her family's poor behaviour that is standing in the way of Jane's happiness. Her father cannot be bothered to check his younger daughter's conduct, her mother does not even realize there is anything wrong with it, and Lydia, in particular, is so self-willed and careless that she is likely to bring shame to the house. The knowledge that her family are so imperfect depresses Elizabeth.

Chapter 38   Elizabeth prepares to leave but not before Mr Collins has the chance to show her just what she has missed by not marrying him. Elizabeth struggles to reply politely. She is still unhappy about Charlotte's position at Hunsford although she sees that her friend is happy. Elizabeth meets with Jane at her aunt's house in London and finds her well. She is anxious to tell Jane about Darcy's proposal, although determined not to hurt her by any reference to Bingley.

Chapter 39   Jane and Elizabeth meet Catherine and Lydia on the last stage of the journey home. Lydia tells them of the times they have enjoyed with the officers and of her desire to go to Brighton to where the officers are decamping. Her increased interest in Wickham is noticed by Elizabeth. This chapter is a prelude to the disastrous event of the elopement of Lydia. On their return home the two elder girls are given a warm welcome. Mr Bennet is particularly pleased to see Elizabeth.

Chapter 40   Elizabeth tells Jane of Darcy's proposal and of his letter. Jane, with her usual desire to see good in everyone, tries to excuse Wickham without blaming Darcy. She finds it difficult to accept Elizabeth's notion that the 'quantity of merit' is only sufficient for one of the men. They cannot both be just and good. Reluctantly they agree they have been taken in by appearances, but decide not to make Wickham's bad character general knowledge – a decision which has dire consequences for the Bennet family. Elizabeth is happier now she has shared her news with Jane but there is one secret (i.e. Bingley) that she has to keep. Mrs Bennet is her usual silly self, both in regard to Jane's situation and also to the Collinses.

Chapter 41   This chapter is concerned chiefly, though separately, with Lydia and Wickham, and can be seen as a prelude to the events that follow. Lydia is determined to go to Brighton. Elizabeth, troubled by the possible dangers of such a visit, tries to persuade her father to ban it. He refuses, believing that Lydia's financial status and the good care of Mrs Lucas will spare her from harm. Elizabeth meets Wickham again. She now sees him in a different light and he seems insincere and affected. She lets him know that she has heard Darcy's side of the story and consequently has changed her view of him. They part with a 'mutual desire of never meeting again'.

Chapter 42   An account of the Bennets' unhappy marriage is an omen for the future attachment of Lydia and Wickham. Elizabeth, far from excusing her father's behaviour, blames him for Lydia's unfortunate conduct. After Wickham's departure, Elizabeth does not feel as happy as she anticipated for life with just her close family seems dull. Instead, she looks forward to the proposed journey with her aunt and uncle, the Gardiners, which, at the last minute, is changed from a tour of the Lake District to a tour of Derbyshire, taking in Pemberley, Darcy's residence.

Chapter 43   At Pemberley, Elizabeth and the Gardiners meet the housekeeper, who paints a fine picture of Darcy. He is a good master, brother and landlord, much to the incredulity of Elizabeth. Musing on this different account of him she comes face to face with the man himself. He, though surprised, is very polite. She, overcome with embarrassment, finds it difficult to talk, so concerned is she that her presence at Pemberley might be considered an impertinence. On meeting again later in the park she is amazed by his civility in wanting to talk to her aunt and uncle, and by his desire that she should meet his sister. Elizabeth is perplexed by the apparent change in his character and confused as to her own feelings towards him.

Chapter 44   Darcy brings his sister and Bingley to see Elizabeth. Miss Darcy is shy but pleasant. Bingley, much to Elizabeth's pleasure, asks about Jane and seems still to be fond of her. It is clear to Mr and Mrs Gardiner that Darcy is in love with Elizabeth. Elizabeth analyses her own feelings towards him. She identifies respect and gratitude but cannot yet admit to love.

Chapter 45   A rather awkward meeting between Elizabeth, the Bingley sisters and Miss Darcy takes place. Elizabeth, still in confusion about her feelings for Darcy, does not know if she wants to meet him or not. Miss Bingley, trying to embarrass Elizabeth with talk of Wickham, does not know how much awkwardness she is causing. When Elizabeth leaves, Miss Bingley tries to blacken her character in front of Darcy and his sister, without success.

Chapter 46   Elizabeth receives two letters from Jane; the first tells her of Lydia and Wickham's elopement, the second reveals the news that they are unlikely to marry. When Darcy is told all this, he becomes very quiet and Elizabeth fears that this is a sign that he has lost interest in her and her family. That thought convinces her of her own feelings for him, and she regrets that her 'love must be in vain'.

Chapter 47   The Gardiners and Elizabeth wonder about the possible whereabouts of the lovers, and are optimistic that they have married in London. Elizabeth, knowing her sister's character and revealing greater knowledge of Wickham's character than she ever has done before, is not optimistic. She regrets she did not make known her knowledge before now. They arrive at Longbourn to hear that Mr Bennet has had no success tracking down the lovers. It is interesting that all the family react in character to the news. Jane, optimistic and benevolent as ever, believes Wickham will marry Lydia. Mrs Bennet bewailing her own personal state, is extreme in her predictions and cares nothing for Lydia herself. Mary makes academic, moral points which reveal no sensitivity or feeling for the distress of the other members of the family. It is left to Mr Gardiner to act with common sense and make practical suggestions.

Chapter 48   Mr Gardiner goes to London to help Mr Bennet search for Lydia. The search is so far unsuccessful and Mr Bennet returns home. Meanwhile they receive a letter from Mr Collins which reveals him in all his selfishness and at his most repellingly pious. Mrs Bennet reacts inconsistently and senselessly to the news of her husband's return. Mr Bennet, although obviously admitting his fault in the situation, cannot shed his flippant attitude to the affair and still manages to joke and tease.

Chapter 49   A letter from Mr Gardiner reveals that Lydia and Wickham have been tracked down and an agreement to marry has been made. Mr Bennet has only to contribute Lydia's share of his bequest, plus one hundred pounds a year. The Bennets assume that Mr Gardiner must have promised Wickham much more than this for him to have agreed to the deal. Mrs Bennet is thrilled with the prospective marriage and gives no thought at all to the circumstances in which it has taken place. It is again left to Elizabeth to observe that although Lydia could not expect much happiness and wealth, it was the best deal she could hope for after the disgrace of the elopement.

Chapter 50   Mr Bennet seeks to find out the amount that he thinks Mr Gardiner has settled on Wickham. Mrs Bennet, with no other thought than for the wedding, is shocked that her husband will not agree to advance Lydia any money for clothes, or allow her to come home on a visit. Elizabeth finally admits that she and Darcy are suited to each other, but regrets that Lydia's marriage will put him off. Mr Gardiner announces that Wickham is to leave his corps and join the regulars and remove to the North. On rational persuasion from Jane and Elizabeth, Mr Bennet relents to allow Lydia to visit home before her departure northwards.

Chapter 51   Lydia and Wickham return to Longbourn, completely without shame and totally unchanged by their experience. Lydia reveals the frivolity of her nature and her insensitivity to all the trouble her family had taken to get her a respectable marriage. She lets it slip that Darcy was present at the wedding. Elizabeth, consumed with curiosity, writes to her aunt to find out why.

Chapter 52   Mrs Gardiner reveals that it was Darcy who paid Wickham the ten thousand pounds. He gave as his reason the guilt he felt in not making Wickham's character publicly known. Mr and Mrs Gardiner suspected there to be another cause which Elizabeth rightly thinks to be herself. She is humbled by the letter and regrets ever being so prejudiced against Darcy. She highly respects him for overcoming his own inherent pride sufficiently to deal so generously with someone he loathes. Yet she feels Darcy would not want to marry her because Wickham is now her brother-in-law. The chapter ends with a conversation between Elizabeth and Wickham in which she subtly lets him know that she is aware of the truth.

Chapter 53 Wickham and Lydia leave for the North. Mrs Bennet's low spirits are revived with the knowledge that Mr Bingley is returning to Netherfield. He calls on them shortly afterwards accompanied by Mr Darcy. Elizabeth is puzzled by his reason for coming, and embarrassed because only she knows what debt they owe him. Her mother reveals her lack of breeding by showing obvious preferential treatment to Bingley, and by her lightly masked insults to Darcy, which only Elizabeth knows are so mistaken. She is pleased to note that Bingley's interest in Jane seems to be increasing again.

Chapter 54 Elizabeth is left to puzzle on Mr Darcy's cool mood and his reason for coming to Longbourn. Her hopes of talking to him and reviving some of the easiness which they felt together at Pemberley are also frustrated when Bingley and he come to dinner on the Tuesday. She has little chance to speak to him and little to say. Jane and Bingley are getting on well although Jane refuses to admit to anything more than friendship between them.

Chapter 55 Darcy returns to London but Bingley continues to call at Longbourn. Rather obviously Mrs Bennet attempts to leave Jane and him alone. Very soon they announce their engagement and the news is greeted with great delight by the family. Even Elizabeth is happy enough to joke about her own spinsterhood and the father is pleased too, although he judges them both to be too kind and compliant to get on in life without the aid of their friends.

Chapter 56 Lady Catherine de Bourgh arrives to interview Elizabeth. She is critical and rude about the size and setting of Longbourn house and garden and proceeds to be equally rude about Elizabeth and her family. She has come to gain confirmation from Elizabeth that she will not marry Darcy; a confirmation that Elizabeth refuses to give. She insists that Darcy is betrothed to her daughter, that Elizabeth's family is too low-class for him and finally the shame of the Wickham/Lydia incident could not allow Darcy to link himself with her. To each accusation Elizabeth answers with strength, reason and dignity. In the end Lady de Bourgh leaves with no satisfactory reply to her question.

Chapter 57 This is a chapter of doubt for Elizabeth and suspense for the reader. Upset by Lady de Bourgh's visit, Elizabeth assumes that she will return to influence Darcy's opinion against her. Her father makes matters worse by treating lightly the rumour that comes from Mr Collins that Elizabeth and Darcy are to be engaged.

Chapter 58 The ends of the plot are being tied. Darcy arrives and during a long walk Darcy and Elizabeth declare their feelings for each other. They talk over their past disagreements and the change in their characters. Both admit to shedding the pride and prejudice which has prevented their friendship beforehand. So all the barriers have been removed and now all that is left is to tell Elizabeth's parents of their proposed marriage.

Chapter 59 Elizabeth breaks the news to her sister and parents. Jane is delighted, though astonished. Her father is reluctant at first, but trusts Elizabeth's judgment on the subject. Mrs Bennet typically sees only the superficial and material advantages and so she too is delighted.

Chaper 60 Darcy explains to Elizabeth that his quietness on his arrival at Longbourn was due to shyness. Lady de Bourgh's intervention, far from putting him off, spurred him on to hope that Elizabeth would accept his proposal the second time. Elizabeth writes to Mrs Gardiner to tell her the glad news. Mr Bennet informs Mr Collins of the forthcoming marriage. Miss Bingley sends her 'insincere' congratulations and Miss Darcy is delighted at the news. Darcy and Elizabeth are both glad that they will not have to stand the vulgar company of some of Elizabeth's relations much longer.

Chapter 61   All the threads are tidily drawn together. Jane and Bingley move to Derbyshire after a year at Netherfield. Kitty's character improves, without the presence of Lydia and under the influence of her elder sisters. Mary, although still inclined to moralize, becomes more sociable now she is no longer in the shadow of her gifted elder sisters. Wickham and Lydia's marriage predictably turns sour and Jane and Elizabeth have to lend them every financial aid they can. Miss Bingley, realizing her interests are more suited by adopting a more pleasant attitude to Jane and Elizabeth, overcomes her jealousy. Georgiana and Elizabeth become very close and are able to live in harmony together at Pemberley. Even Lady de Bourgh despite her tremendous hostility at first, swallows her pride and agrees eventually to visit Pemberley. The Gardiners become firm friends, Darcy ever grateful to them for bringing Elizabeth to Pemberley.

Coursework and preparing for the examination

If you wish to gain a certificate in English literature then there is no substitute for studying the text/s on which you are to be examined. If you cannot be bothered to do that, then neither this guide nor any other will be of use to you.

Here we give advice on studying the text, writing a good essay, producing coursework, and sitting the examination. However, if you meet problems you should ask your teacher for help.

Studying the text

No, not just read – study. You must read your text at least twice. Do not dismiss it if you find a first reading difficult or uninteresting. Approach the text with an open mind and you will often find a second reading more enjoyable. When you become a more experienced reader enjoyment usually follows from a close study of the text, when you begin to appreciate both what the author is saying and the skill with which it is said.

Having read the text, you must now study it. We restrict our remarks here to novels and plays, though much of what is said can also be applied to poetry.

1 You will know in full detail all the major incidents in your text, **why**, **where** and **when** they happen, **who** is involved, **what** leads up to them and what follows.

2 You must show that you have an **understanding of the story**, the **characters**, and the **main ideas** which the author is exploring.

3 In a play you must know what happens in each act, and more specifically the organization of the scene structure – how one follows from and builds upon another. Dialogue in both plays and novels is crucial. You must have a detailed knowledge of the major dialogues and soliloquies and the part they play in the development of plot, and the development and drawing of character.

4 When you write about a novel you will not normally be expected to quote or to refer to specific lines but references to incidents and characters must be given, and they must be accurate and specific.

5 In writing about a play you will be expected both to paraphrase dialogue and quote specific lines, always provided, of course, that they are actually contributing something to your essay!

To gain full marks in coursework and/or in an examination you will also be expected to show your own reaction to, and appreciation of, the text studied. The teacher or examiner always welcomes those essays which demonstrate the student's own thoughtful response to the text. Indeed, questions often specify such a requirement, so do participate in those classroom discussions, the debates, class dramatizations of all or selected parts of your text, and the many other activities which enable a class to share and grow in their understanding and feeling for literature.

Making notes
A half-hearted reading of your text, or watching the 'film of the book' will not give you the necessary knowledge to meet the above demands.

As you study the text jot down sequences of events; quotations of note; which events precede and follow the part you are studying; the characters involved; what the part being studied contributes to the plot and your understanding of character and ideas.

Write single words, phrases and short sentences which can be quickly reviewed and which will help you to gain a clear picture of the incident being studied. Make your notes neat and orderly, with headings to indicate chapter, scene, page, incident, character, etc, so that you can quickly find the relevant notes or part of the text when revising.

Writing the essay

Good essays are like good books, in miniature; they are thought about, planned, logically structured, paragraphed, have a clearly defined pattern and development of thought, and are presented clearly – and with neat writing! All of this will be to no avail if the tools you use, i.e. words, and the skill with which you put them together to form your sentences and paragraphs are severely limited.

How good is your general and literary vocabulary? Do you understand and can you make appropriate use of such terms as 'soliloquy', 'character', 'plot', 'mood', 'dramatically effective', 'comedy', 'allusion', 'humour', 'imagery', 'irony', 'paradox', 'anti-climax', 'tragedy'? These are all words which examiners have commented on as being misunderstood by students.

Do you understand 'metaphor', 'simile', 'alliteration'? Can you say what their effect is on you, the reader, and how they enable the author to express himself more effectively than by the use of a different literary device? If you cannot, you are employing your time ineffectively by using them.

You are writing an English literature essay and your writing should be literate and appropriate. Slang, colloquialisms and careless use of words are not tolerated in such essays.

Essays for coursework

The exact number of essays you will have to produce and their length will vary; it depends upon the requirements of the examination board whose course you are following, and whether you will be judged solely on coursework or on a mixture of coursework and examination.

As a guide, however your course is structured, you will be required to provide a folder containing at least ten essays, and from that folder approximately five will be selected for moderation purposes. Of those essays, one will normally have been done in class-time under conditions similar to those of an examination. The essays must cover the complete range of course requirements and be the unaided work of the student. One board specifies that these pieces of continuous writing should be a minimum of 400 words long, and another, a minimum of 500 words long. Ensure that you know what is required for your course, and do not aim for the minimum amount – write a full essay then prune it down if necessary.

Do take care over the presentation of your final folder of coursework. There are many devices on the market which will enable you to bind your work neatly, and in such a way that you can easily insert new pieces. Include a 'Contents' page and a front and back cover to keep your work clean. Ring binders are unsuitable items to hand in for **final** assessment purposes as they are much too bulky.

What sort of coursework essays will you be set? All boards lay down criteria similar to the following for the range of student response to literature that the coursework must cover.

Work must demonstrate that the student:

1 shows an understanding not only of surface meaning but also of a deeper awareness of themes and attitudes;

2 recognizes and appreciates ways in which authors use language;

3 recognizes and appreciates ways in which writers achieve their effects, particularly in how the work is structured and in its characterization;

4 can write imaginatively in exploring and developing ideas so as to communicate a sensitive and informed personal response to what is read.

Much of what is said in the section **'Writing essays in an examination'** (below) is relevant here, but for coursework essays you have the advantage of plenty of time to prepare your work – so take advantage of it.

There is no substitute for arguing, discussing and talking about a question on a particular text or theme. Your teacher should give you plenty of opportunity for this in the classroom. Listening to what others say about a subject often opens up for you new ways to look at and respond to it. The same can be said for reading about a topic. Be careful not to copy down slavishly what others say and write. Jot down notes then go away and think about what you have heard, read and written. Make more notes of your own and then start to clarify your own thoughts, feelings and emotions on the subject about which you are writing. Most students make the mistake of doing their coursework essays in a rush – you have time so use it.

Take a great deal of care in planning your work. From all your notes, write a rough draft and then start the task of really perfecting it.

1 Look at your arrangement of paragraphs, is there a logical development of thought or argument? Do the paragraphs need rearranging in order? Does the first or last sentence of any paragraph need redrafting in order to provide a sensible link with the preceding or next paragraph?

2 Look at the pattern of sentences within each paragraph. Are your thoughts and ideas clearly developed and expressed? Have you used any quotations, paraphrases, or references to incidents to support your opinions and ideas? Are those references relevant and apt, or just 'padding'?

3 Look at the words you have used. Try to avoid repeating words in close proximity one to another. Are the words you have used to comment on the text being studied the most appropriate and effective, or just the first ones you thought of?

4 Check your spelling and punctuation.

5 Now write a final draft, the quality of which should reflect the above considerations.

Writing essays in an examination
Read the question. Identify the key words and phrases. Write them down, and as they are dealt with in your essay plan, tick them off.

Plan your essay. Spend about five minutes jotting down ideas; organize your thoughts and ideas into a logical and developing order – a structure is essential to the production of a good essay. Remember, brief, essential notes only!

Write your essay
How long should it be? There is no magic length. What you must do is answer the question set, fully and sensitively in the time allowed. You will probably have about forty minutes to answer an essay question, and within that time you should produce an essay between roughly 350 and 500 words in length. Very short answers will not do justice to the question, very long answers will probably contain much irrelevant information and waste time that should be spent on the next answer.

How much quotation? Use only that which is apt and contributes to the clarity and quality of your answer. No examiner will be impressed by 'padding'.

What will the examiners be looking for in an essay?
1 An answer to the question set, and not a prepared answer to another, albeit slightly similar question done in class.

2 A well-planned, logically structured and paragraphed essay with a beginning, middle and end.

3 Accurate references to plot, character, theme, as required by the question.

4 Appropriate, brief, and if needed, frequent quotation and references to support and demonstrate the comments that you are making in your essay.

5 Evidence that reading the text has prompted in you a personal response to it, as well as some judgment and appreciation of its literary merit.

How do you prepare to do this?
1 During your course you should write between three to five essays on each text.

2 Make good use of class discussion etc, as mentioned in a previous paragraph on page 75.

3 Try to see a live performance of a play. It may help to see a film of a play or book, though be aware that directors sometimes leave out episodes, change their order, or worse, add episodes that are not in the original – so be very careful. In the end, there is no substitute for **reading and studying** the text!

Try the following exercises without referring to any notes or text.

1 Pick a character from your text.

2 Make a list of his/her qualities – both positive and negative ones, or aspects that you cannot quite define. Jot down single words to describe each quality. If you do not know the word you want, use a thesaurus, but use it in conjunction with a dictionary and make sure you are fully aware of the meaning of each word you use.

3 Write a short sentence which identifies one or more places in the text where you think each quality is demonstrated.

4 Jot down any brief quotation, paraphrase of conversation or outline of an incident which shows that quality.

5 Organize the list. Identify groupings which contrast the positive and negative aspects of character.

6 Write a description of that character which makes full use of the material you have just prepared.

7 What do you think of the character you have just described? How has he/she reacted to and coped with the pressures of the other characters, incidents, and the setting of the story? Has he/she changed in any way? In no more than 100 words, including 'evidence' taken from the text, write a balanced assessment of the character, and draw some conclusions.

You should be able to do the above without notes, and without the text, unless you are to take an examination which allows the use of plain texts. In plain text examinations you are allowed to take in a copy of your text. It must be without notes, either your own or the publisher's. The intention is to enable you to consult a text in the examination so as to confirm memory of detail, thus enabling a candidate to quote and refer more accurately in order to illustrate his/her views that more effectively. Examiners will expect a high standard of accurate reference, quotation and comment in a plain text examination.

Sitting the examination

You will have typically between two and five essays to write and you will have roughly 40 minutes, on average, to write each essay.

On each book you have studied, you should have a choice of doing at least one out of two or three essay titles set.

1 **Before sitting the exam**, make sure you are completely clear in your mind that you know exactly how many questions you must answer, which sections of the paper you must tackle, and how many questions you may, or must, attempt on any one book or in any one section of the paper. If you are not sure, ask your teacher.

2 **Always read the instructions** given at the top of your examination paper. They are

there to help you. Take your time, and try to relax – panicking will not help.

3 Be very clear about timing, and organizing your time

(a) Know how long the examination is.

(b) Know how many questions you must do.

(c) Divide (b) into (a) to work out how long you may spend on each question. (Bear in mind that some questions may attract more marks, and should therefore take proportionately more time.)

(d) Keep an eye on the time, and do not spend more than you have allowed for any one question.

(e) If you have spare time at the end you can come back to a question and do more work on it.

(f) Do not be afraid to jot down notes as an aid to memory, but do cross them out carefully after use – a single line will do!

4 Do not rush the decision as to which question you are going to answer on a particular text.

(a) Study each question carefully.

(b) Be absolutely sure what each one is asking for.

(c) Make your decision as to which you will answer.

5 Having decided which question you will attempt:

(a) jot down the key points of the actual question – use single words or short phrases.

(b) think about how you are going to arrange your answer. Five minutes here, with some notes jotted down will pay dividends later.

(c) write your essay, and keep an eye on the time!

6 Adopt the same approach for all questions. Do write answers for the maximum number of questions you are told to attempt. One left out will lose its proportion of the total marks. Remember also, you will never be awarded extra marks, over and above those already allocated, if you write an extra long essay on a particular question.

7 Do not waste time on the following:

(a) an extra question – you will get no marks for it.

(b) worrying about how much anyone else is writing, they can't help you!

(c) relaxing at the end with time to spare – you do not have any. Work up to the very moment the invigilator tells you to stop writing. Check and recheck your work, including spelling and punctuation. Every single mark you gain helps, and that last mark might tip the balance between success and failure – the line has to be drawn somewhere.

8 Help the examiner.

(a) Do not use red or green pen or pencil on your paper. Examiners usually annotate your script in red and green, and if you use the same colours it will cause unnecessary confusion.

(b) Leave some space between each answer or section of an answer. This could also help you if you remember something you wish to add to your answer when you are checking it.

(c) Number your answers as instructed. If it is question 3 you are doing, do not label it 'C'.

(d) Write neatly. It will help you to communicate effectively with the examiner who is trying to read your script.

Glossary of literary terms

Mere knowledge of the words in this list or other specialist words used when studying literature is not sufficient. You must know when to use a particular term, and be able to describe what it contributes to that part of the work which is being discussed.

For example, merely to label something as being a metaphor does not help an examiner or teacher to assess your response to the work being studied. You must go on to analyse what the literary device contributes to the work. Why did the author use a metaphor at all? Why not some other literary device? What extra sense of feeling or meaning does the metaphor convey to the reader? How effective is it in supporting the author's intention? What was the author's intention, as far as you can judge, in using that metaphor?

Whenever you use a particular literary term you must do so with a purpose and that purpose usually involves an explanation and expansion upon its use. Occasionally you will simply use a literary term 'in passing', as, for example, when you refer to the 'narrator' of a story as opposed to the 'author' – they are not always the same! So please be sure that you understand both the meaning and purpose of each literary term you employ.

This list includes only those words which we feel will assist in helping you to understand the major concepts in play and novel construction. It makes no attempt to be comprehensive. These are the concepts which examiners frequently comment upon as being inadequately grasped by many students. Your teacher will no doubt expand upon this list and introduce you to other literary devices and words within the context of the particular work/s you are studying – the most useful place to experience and explore them and their uses.

Plot This is the plan or story of a play or novel. Just as a body has a skeleton to hold it together, so the plot forms the 'bare bones' of the work of literature in play or novel form. It is however, much more than this. It is arranged in time, so one of the things which encourages us to continue reading is to see what happens next. It deals with causality, that is how one event or incident causes another. It has a sequence, so that in general, we move from the beginning through to the end.

Structure The arrangement and interrelationship of parts in a play or novel are obviously bound up with the plot. An examination of how the author has structured his work will lead us to consider the function of, say, the 43 letters which are such an important part of *Pride and Prejudice*. We would consider the arrangement of the time-sequence in *Wuthering Heights* with its 'flashbacks' and their association with the different narrators of the story. In a play we would look at the scene divisions and how different events are placed in a relationship so as to produce a particular effect; where soliloquies occur so as to inform the audience of a character's innermost emotions and feelings. Do be aware that great works of fiction are not just simply thrown together by their authors. We study a work in detail, admiring its parts and the intricacies of its structure. The reason for a work's greatness has to do with the genius of its author and the care of its construction. Ultimately, though, we do well to remember that it is the work as a whole that we have to judge, not just the parts which make up that whole.

Narrator
A narrator tells or relates a story. In *Wuthering Heights* various characters take on the task of narrating the events of the story: Cathy, Heathcliff, etc, as well as being, at other times, central characters taking their part in the story. Sometimes the author will be there, as it were, in person, relating and explaining events. The method adopted in telling the story relates very closely to style and structure.

Style
The manner in which something is expressed or performed, considered as separate from its intrinsic content or meaning. It might well be that a lyrical, almost poetical style will be used, for example concentrating on the beauties and contrasts of the natural world as a foil to the narration of the story and creating emotions in the reader which serve to heighten reactions to the events being played out on the page. It might be that the author uses a terse, almost staccato approach to the conveyance of his story. There is no simple route to grasping the variations of style which are to be found between different authors or indeed within one novel. The surest way to appreciate this difference is to read widely and thoughtfully and to analyse and appreciate the various strategies which an author uses to command our attention.

Character
A person represented in a play or story. However, the word also refers to the combination of traits and qualities distinguishing the individual nature of a person or thing. Thus, a characteristic is one such distinguishing quality: in *Pride and Prejudice*, the pride and prejudices of various characters are central to the novel, and these characteristics which are associated with Mr Darcy, Elizabeth, and Lady Catherine in that novel, enable us to begin assessing how a character is reacting to the surrounding events and people. Equally, the lack of a particular trait or characteristic can also tell us much about a character.

Character development
In *Pride and Prejudice*, the extent to which Darcy's pride, or Elizabeth's prejudice is altered, the recognition by those characters of such change, and the events of the novel which bring about the changes are central to any exploration of how a character develops, for better or worse.

Irony
This is normally taken to be the humorous or mildly sarcastic use of words to imply the opposite of what they say. It also refers to situations and events and thus you will come across references such as prophetic, tragic, and dramatic irony.

Dramatic irony
This occurs when the implications of a situation or speech are understood by the audience but not by all or some of the characters in the play or novel. We also class as ironic words spoken innocently but which a later event proves either to have been mistaken or to have prophesied that event. When we read in the play *Macbeth*:

> *Macbeth*
> Tonight we hold a solemn supper, sir,
> And I'll request your presence.

> *Banquo*
> Let your highness
> Command upon me, to the which my duties
> Are with a most indissoluble tie
> Forever knit.

we, as the audience, will shortly have revealed to us the irony of Macbeth's words. He does not expect Banquo to attend the supper as he plans to have Banquo murdered before the supper occurs. However, what Macbeth does not know is the prophetic irony of Banquo's response. His 'duties. . . a most indissoluble tie' will be fulfilled by his appearance at the supper as a ghost – something Macbeth certainly did not forsee or welcome, and which Banquo most certainly did not have in mind!

Tragedy
This is usually applied to a play in which the main character, usually a person of importance and outstanding personal qualities, falls to disaster through the combination of personal failing and circumstances with which he cannot deal. Such tragic happenings may also be central to a novel. In *The Mayor of Casterbridge*, flaws in Henchard's character are partly responsible for his downfall and eventual death.

In Shakespeare's plays, *Macbeth* and *Othello*, the tragic heroes from which the two plays take their names, are both highly respected and honoured men who have proven their outstanding personal qualities. Macbeth, driven on by his ambition and that of his very determined wife, kills his king. It leads to civil war in his country, to his own eventual downfall and death, and to his wife's suicide. Othello, driven to an insane jealousy by the cunning of his lieutenant, Iago, murders his own innocent wife and commits suicide.

Satire   Where topical issues, folly or evil are held up to scorn by means of ridicule and irony – the satire may be subtle or openly abusive.

In *Animal Farm*, George Orwell used the rebellion of the animals against their oppressive owner to satirize the excesses of the Russian revolution at the beginning of the 20th century. It would be a mistake, however, to see the satire as applicable only to that event. There is a much wider application of that satire to political and social happenings both before and since the Russian revolution and in all parts of the world.

Images   An image is a mental representation or picture. One that constantly recurs in *Macbeth* is clothing, sometimes through double meanings of words: 'he seems rapt withal', 'Why do you dress me in borrowed robes?', 'look how our partner's rapt', 'Like our strange garments, cleave not to their mould', 'Whiles I stood rapt in the wonder of it', 'which would be worn now in their newest gloss', 'Was the hope drunk Wherein you dressed yourself?', 'Lest our old robes sit easier than our new.', 'like a giant's robe upon a dwarfish thief'. All these images serve to highlight and comment upon aspects of Macbeth's behaviour and character. In Act 5, Macbeth the loyal soldier who was so honoured by his king at the start of the play, struggles to regain some small shred of his self-respect. Three times he calls to Seyton for his armour, and finally moves toward his destiny with the words 'Blow wind, come wrack, At least we'll die with harness on our back' – his own armour, not the borrowed robes of a king he murdered.

Do remember that knowing a list of images is not sufficient. You must be able to interpret them and comment upon the contribution they make to the story being told.

Theme   A unifying idea, image or motif, repeated or developed throughout a work.

In *Pride and Prejudice*, a major theme is marriage. During the course of the novel we are shown various views of and attitudes towards marriage. We actually witness the relationships of four different couples through their courtship, engagement and eventual marriage. Through those events and the examples presented to us in the novel of other already married couples, the author engages in a thorough exploration of the theme.

This list is necessarily short. There are whole books devoted to the explanation of literary terms. Some concepts, like style, need to be experienced and discussed in a group setting with plenty of examples in front of you. Others, such as dramatic irony, need keen observation from the student and a close knowledge of the text to appreciate their significance and existence. All such specialist terms are well worth knowing. But they should be used only if they enable you to more effectively express your knowledge and appreciation of the work being studied.